# DON'T GO OUTSIDE

TOKYO STREET PHOTOS

SEAN BONNER

SURPRISE
ATTACK

Published by Surprise Attack Press
ISBN 978-0-9898144-3-0
surpriseattack.net



First Printing: 2017

Sean Bonner
seanbonner.com

Prints available at seanbonner.photos

*Surrounded by*
*my solitude*
*alone in the dark*
*never felt so good*
– Deadguy

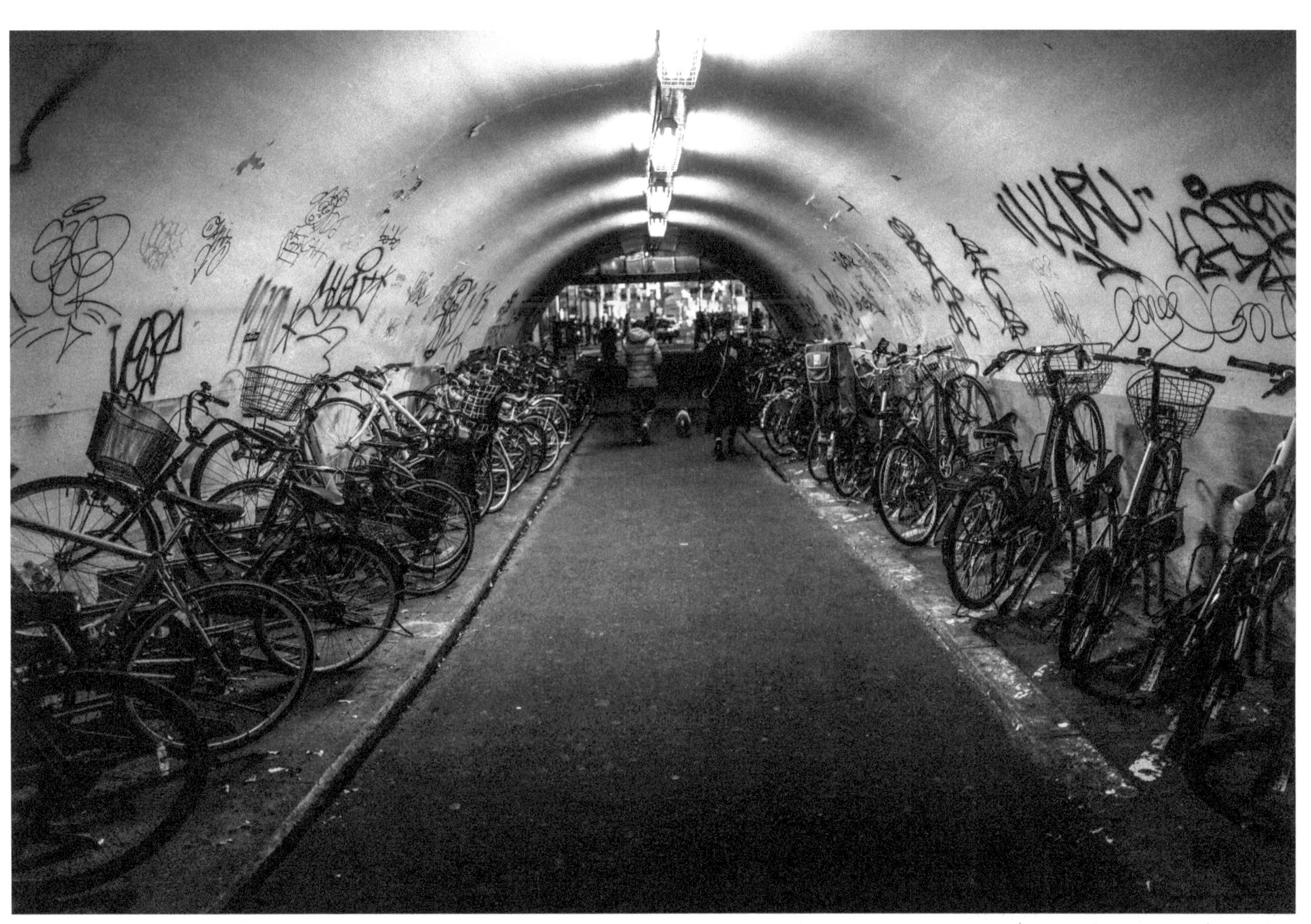

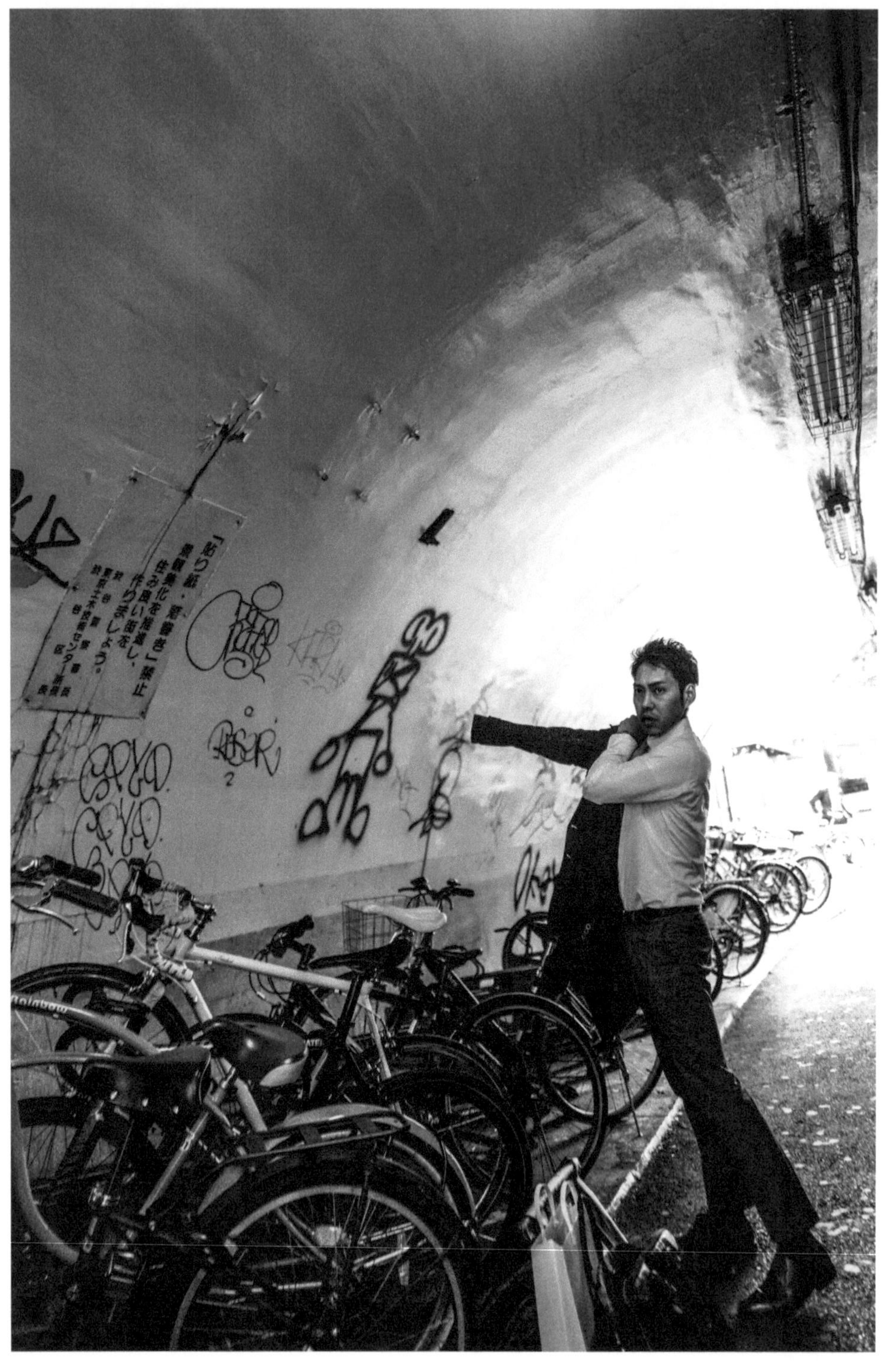
「貼り紙・落書き」禁止
景観美化を推進し、
住み良い街を
作りましょう。

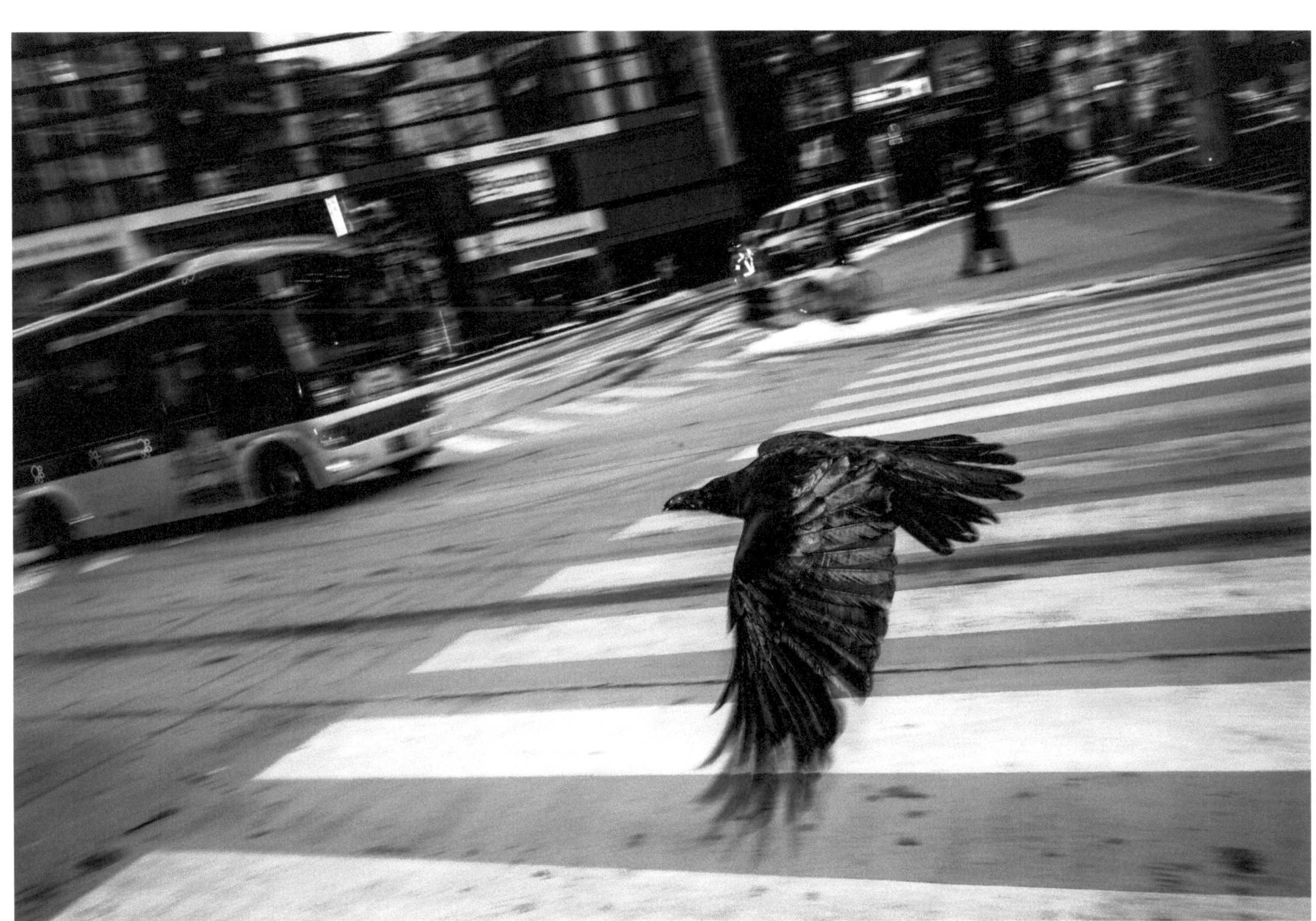

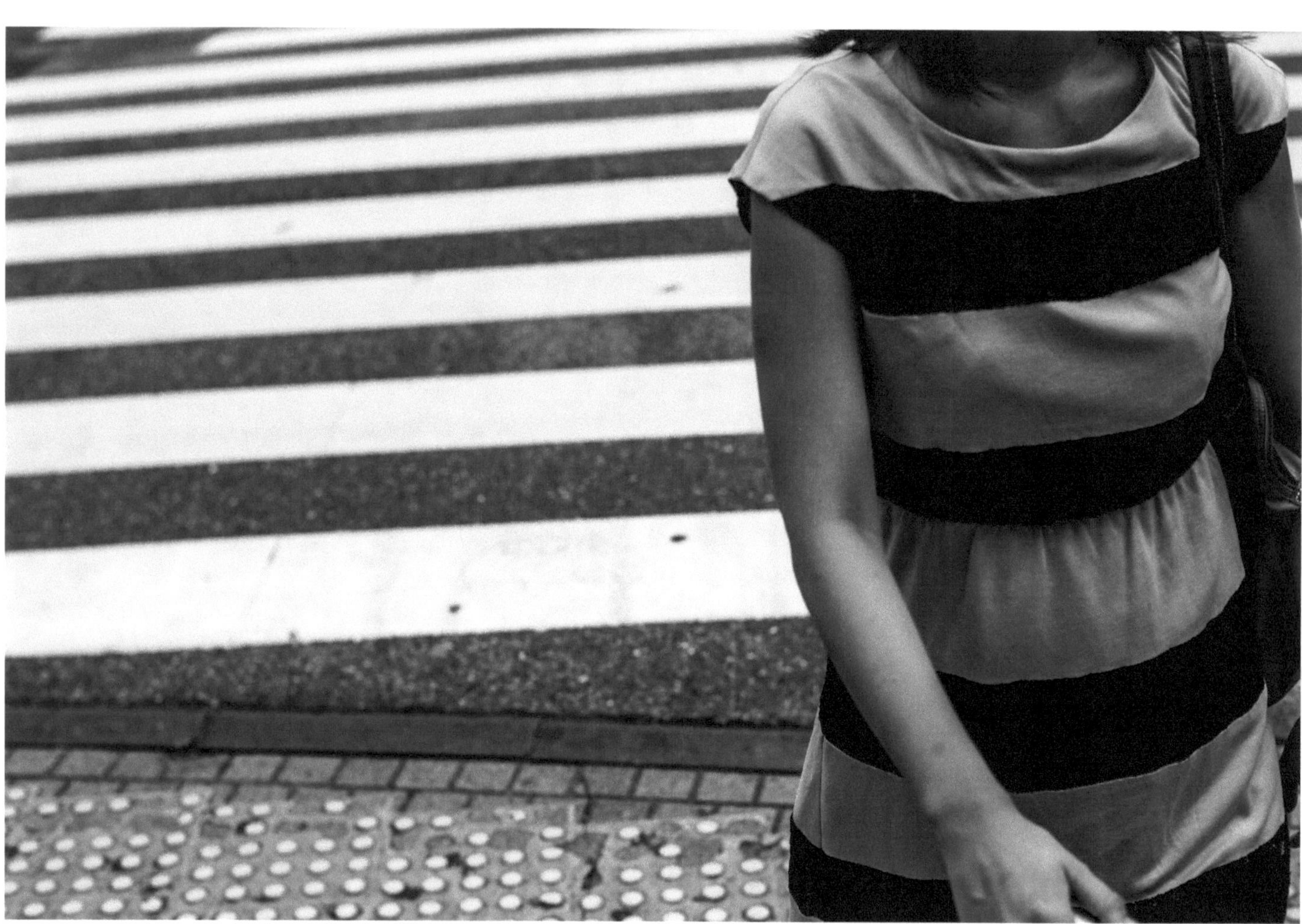

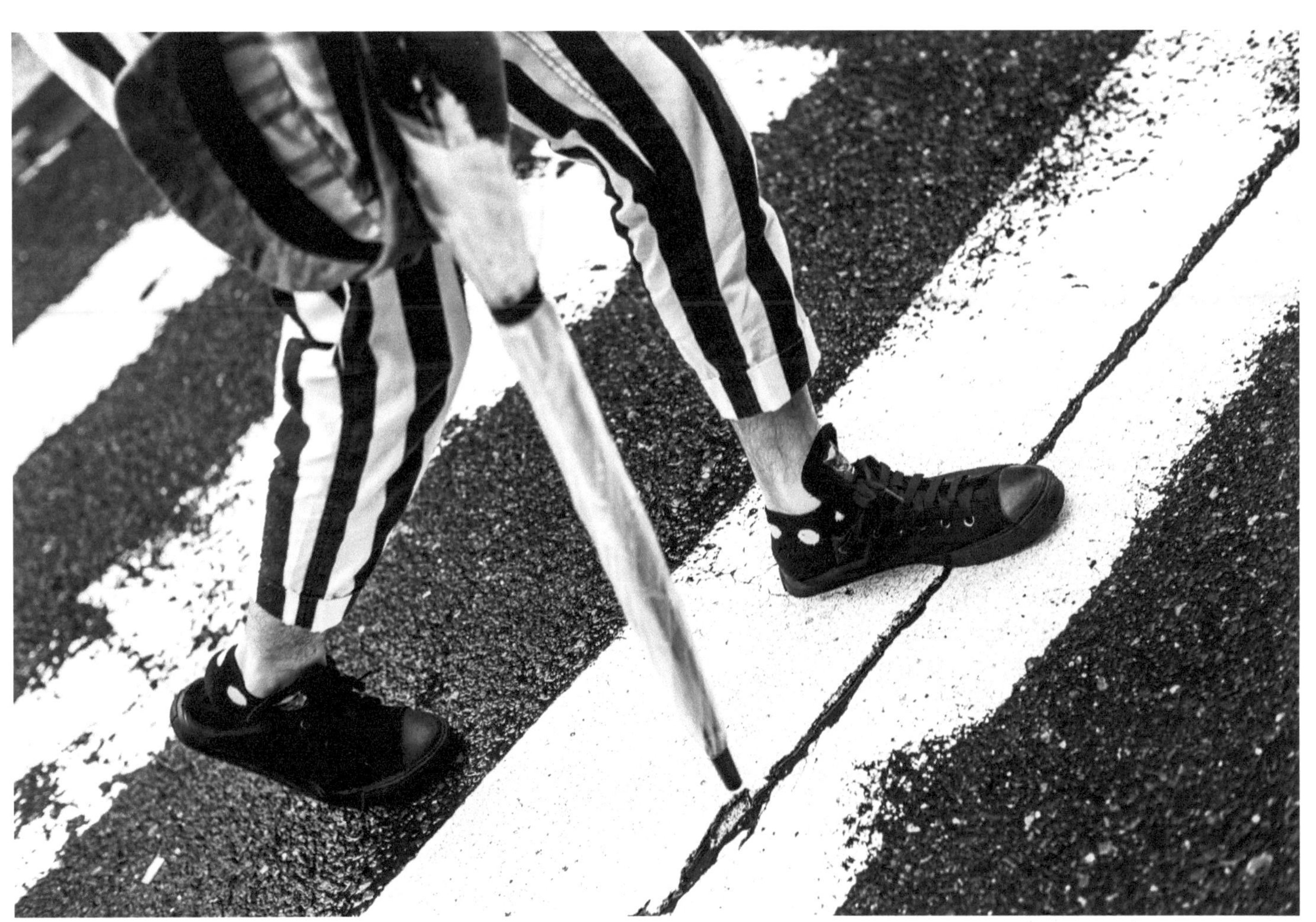

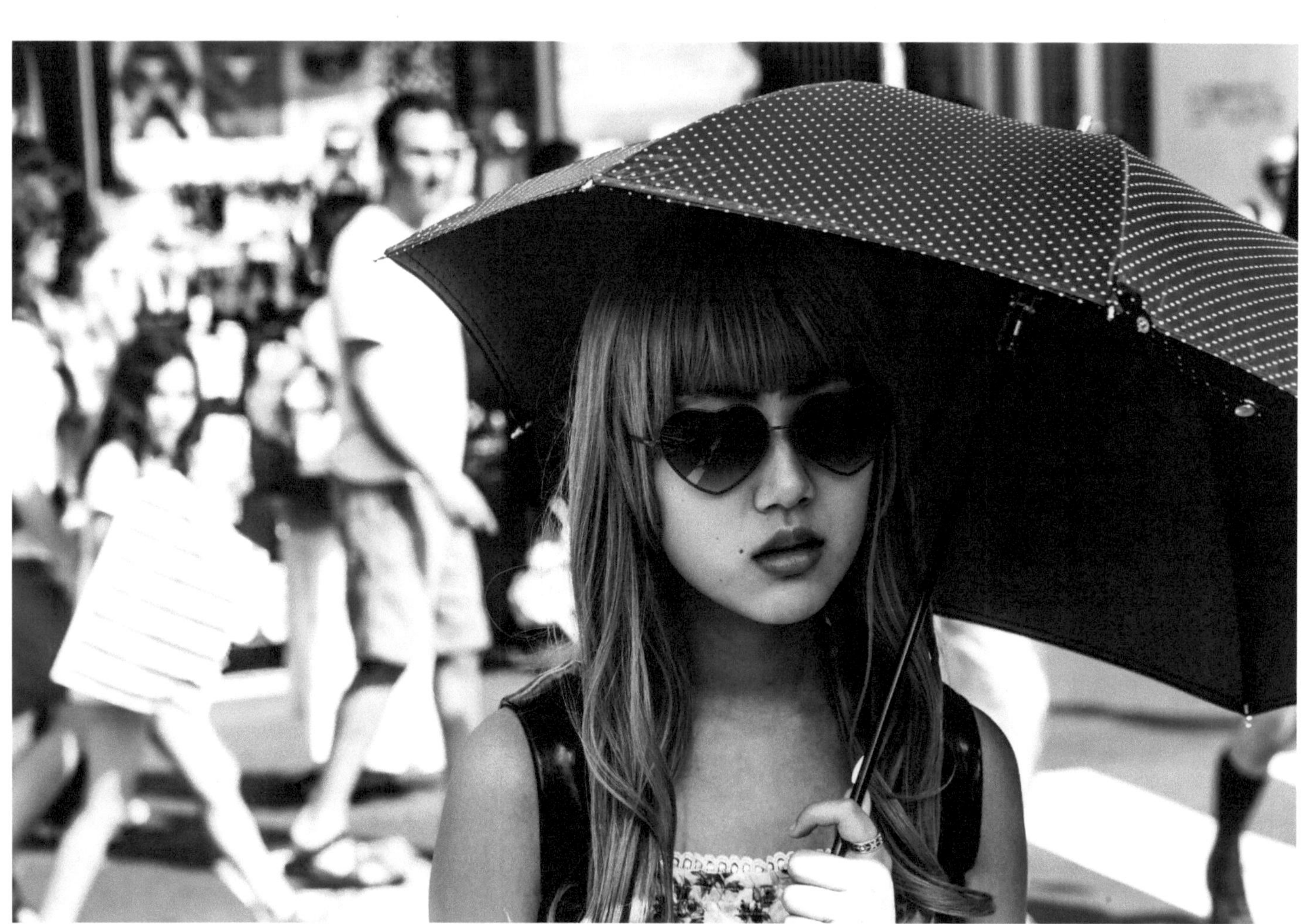

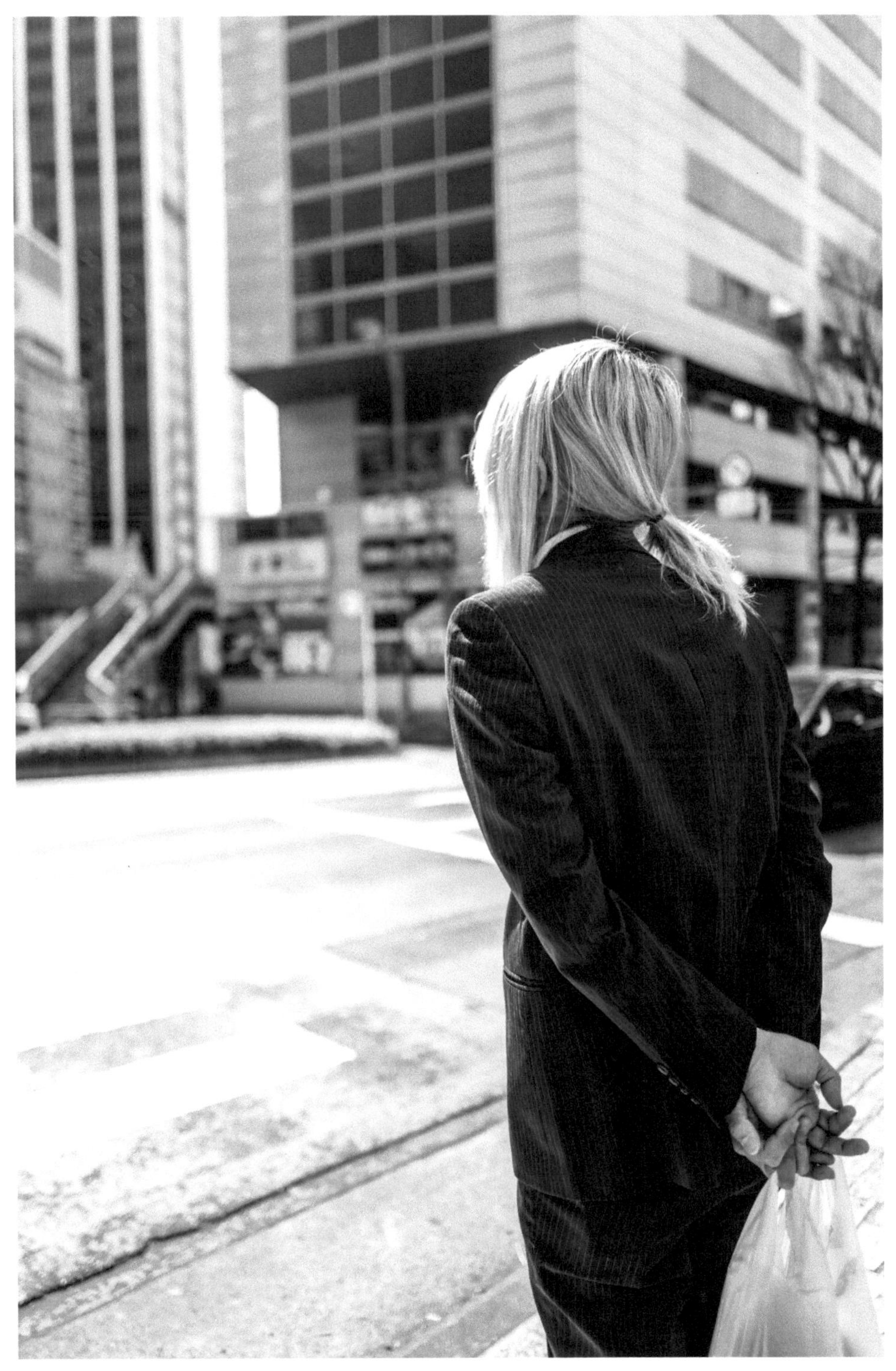

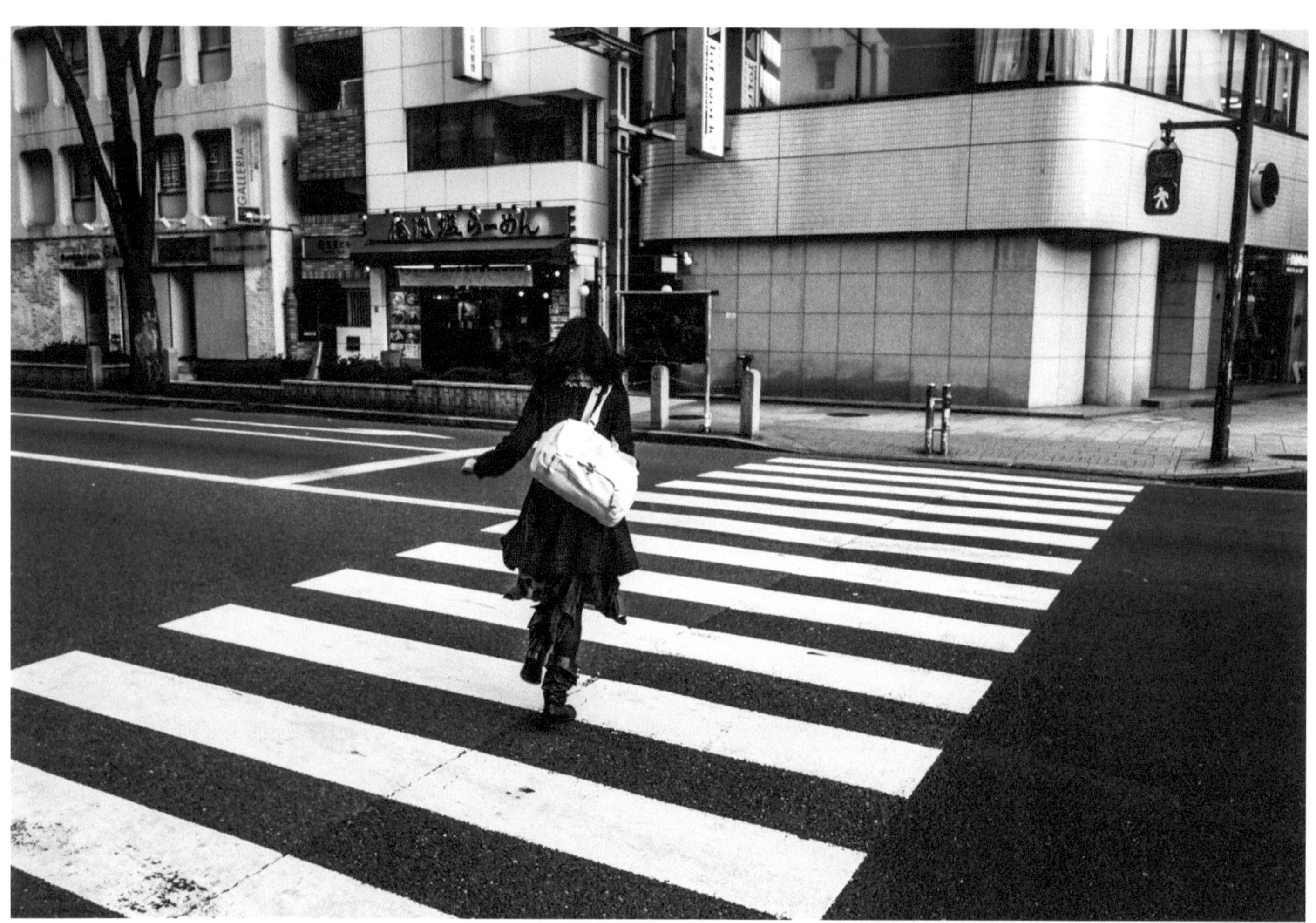
GALLERIA

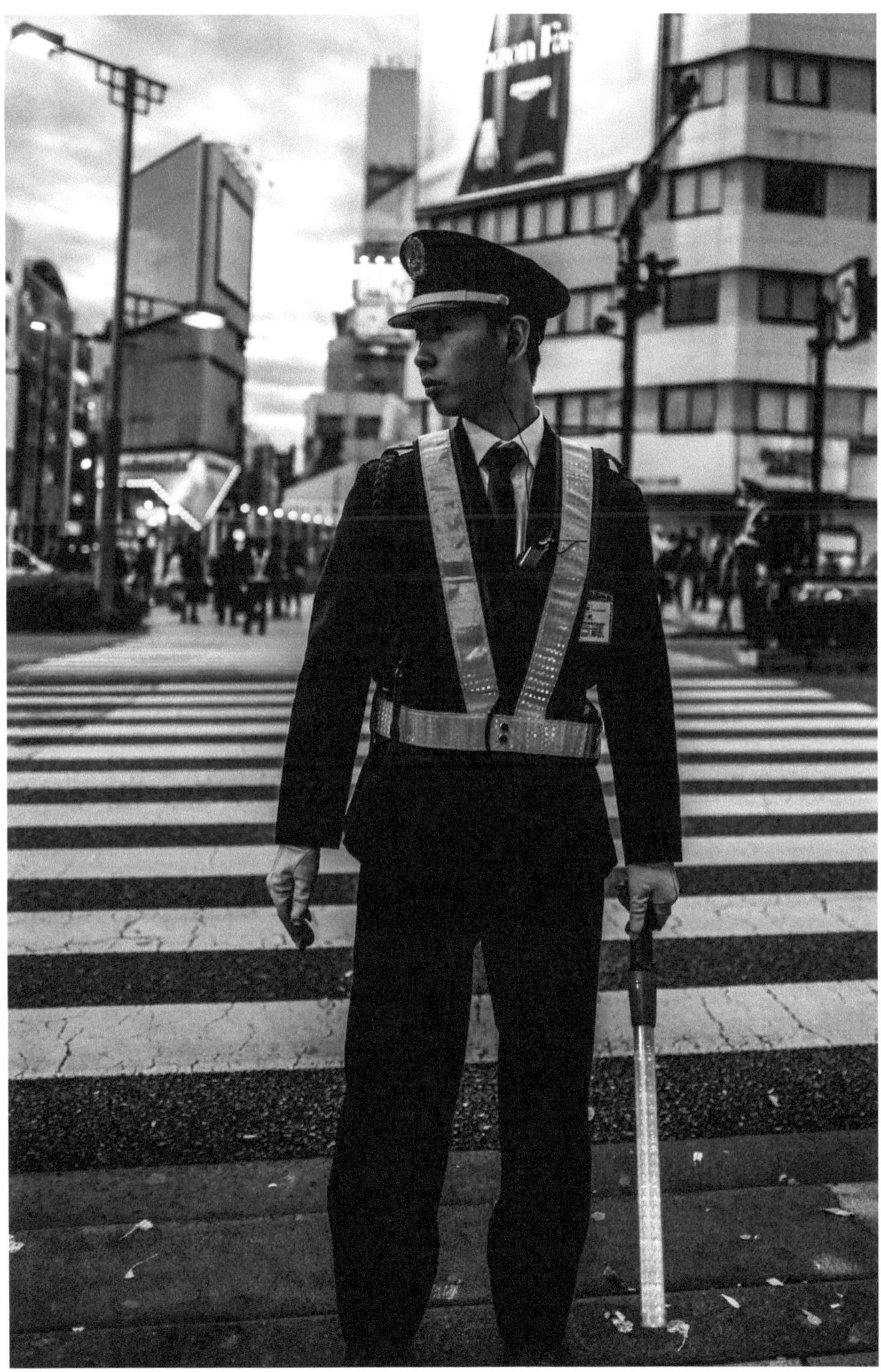

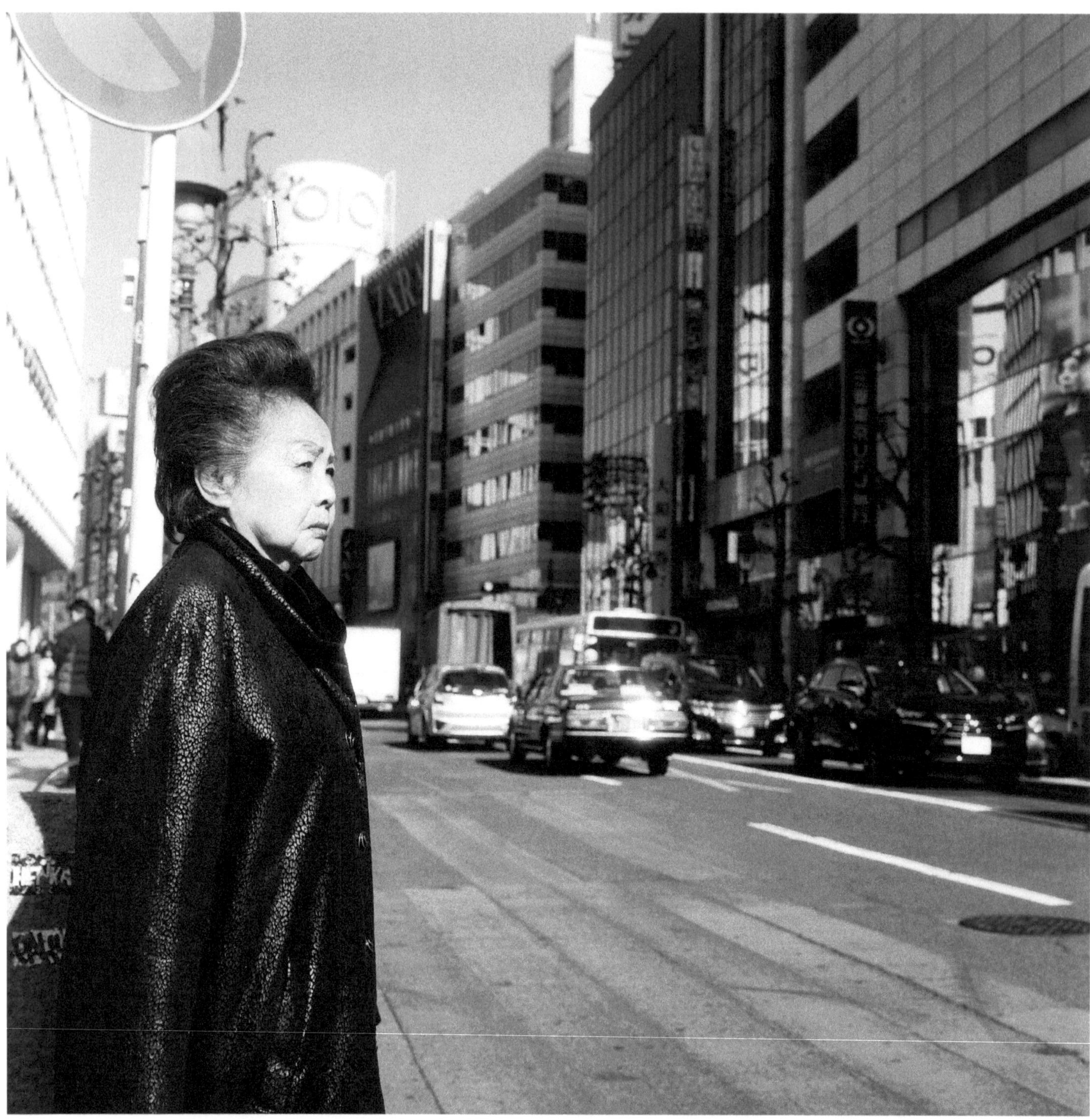

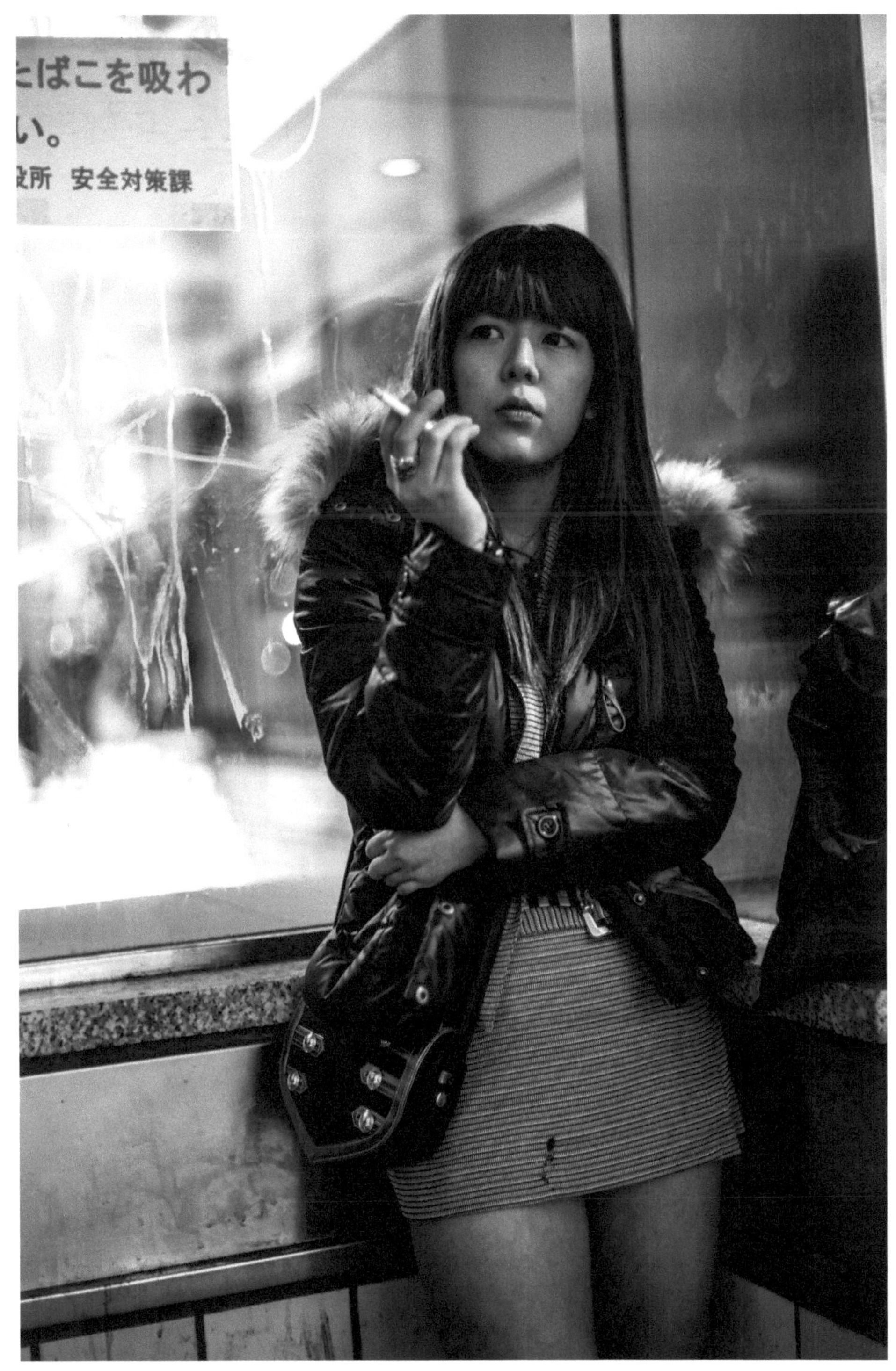
ばこを吸わ
い。
所　安全対策課

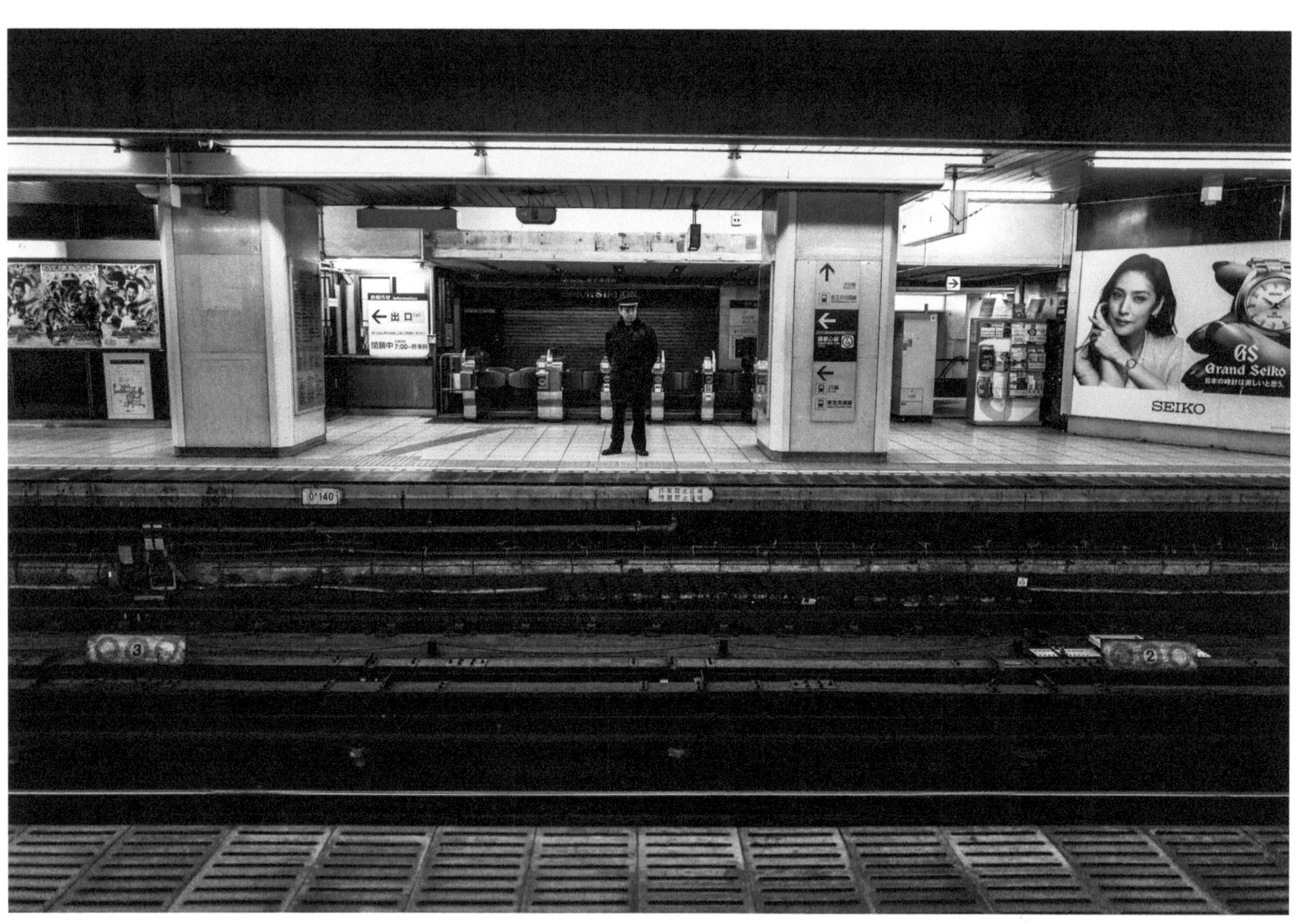
出口
GS
Grand Seiko
日本の時計は美しいと思う。
SEIKO
0'140
3
2

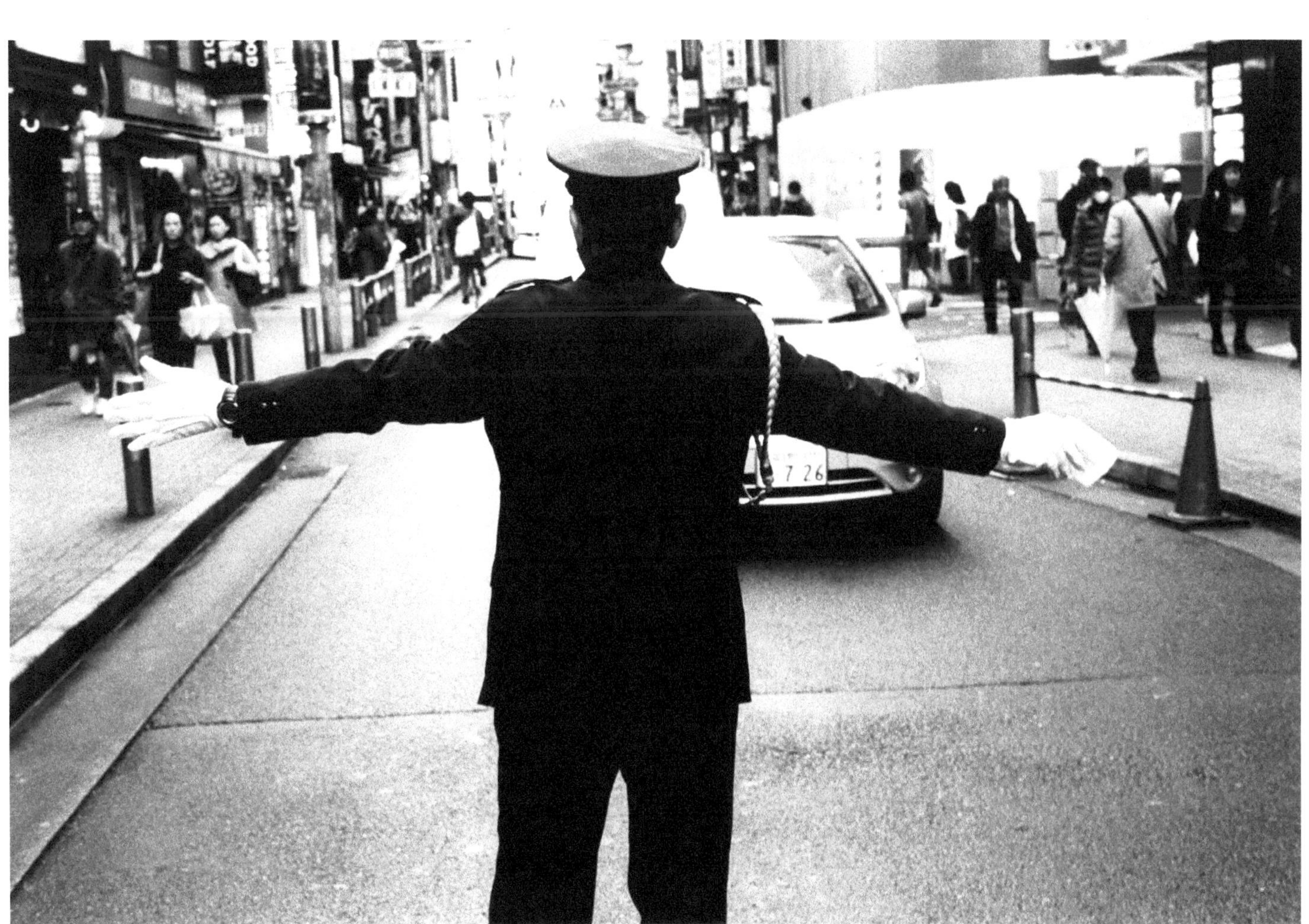

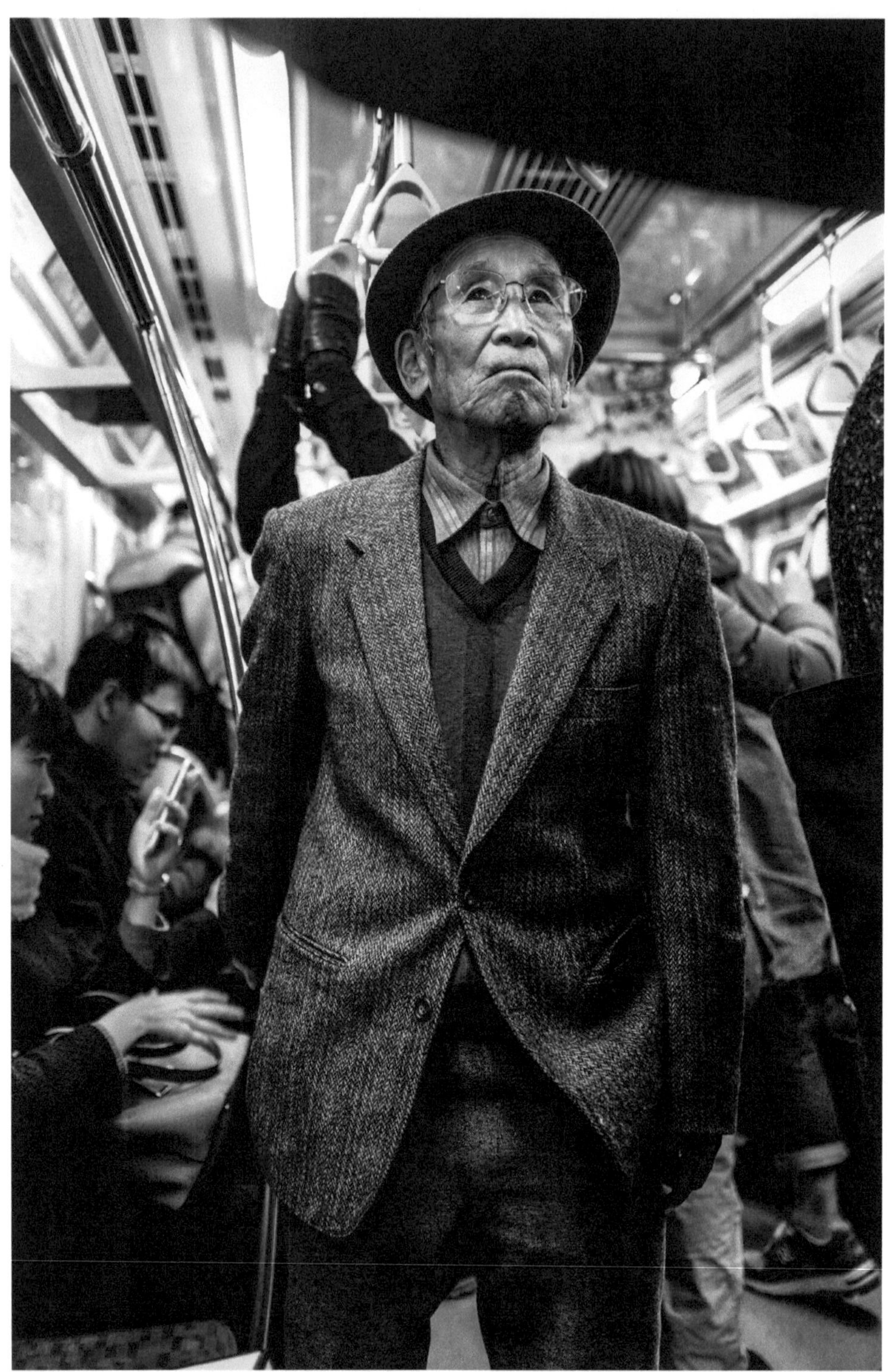

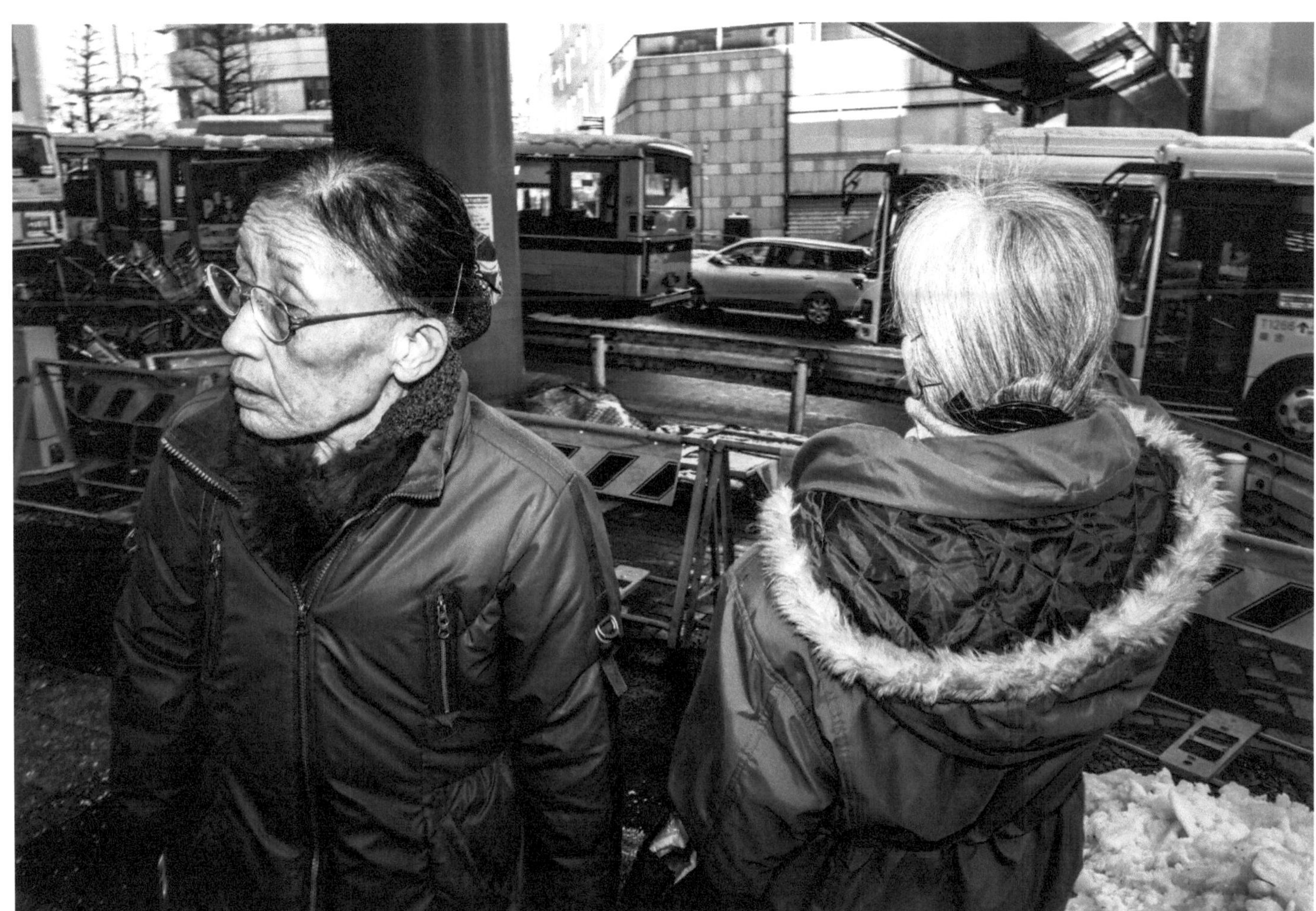

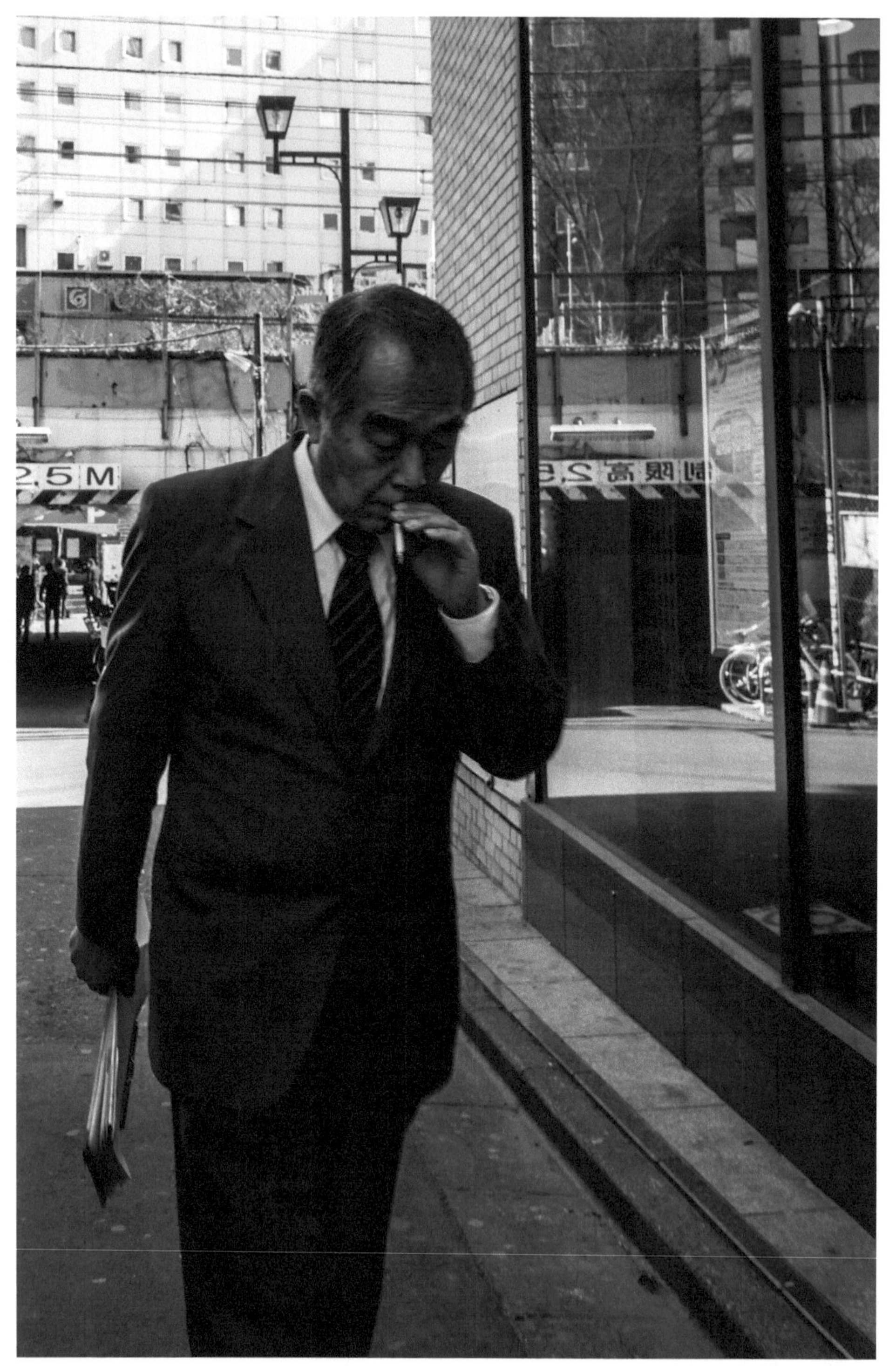
2.5M

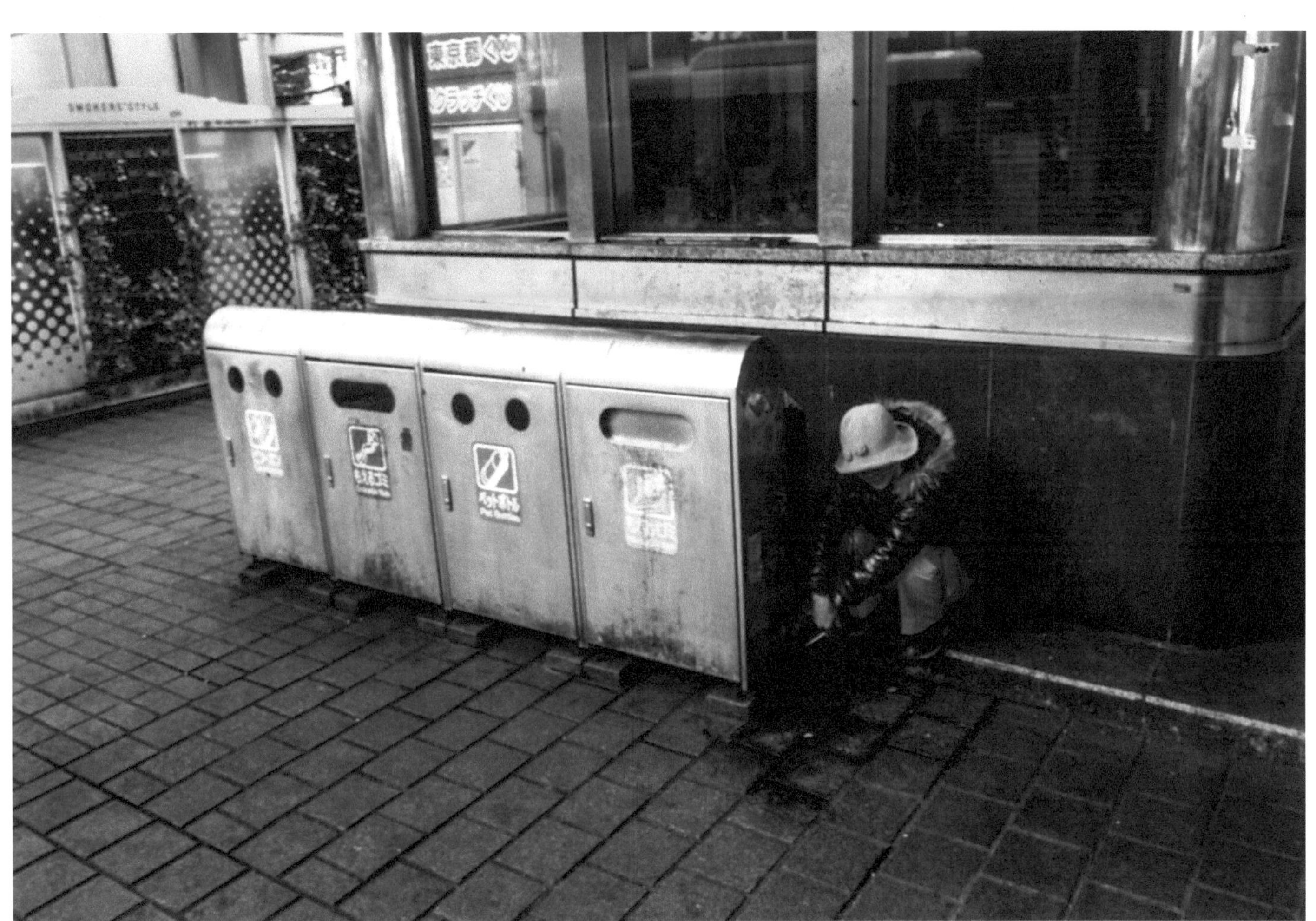
東京都くじ

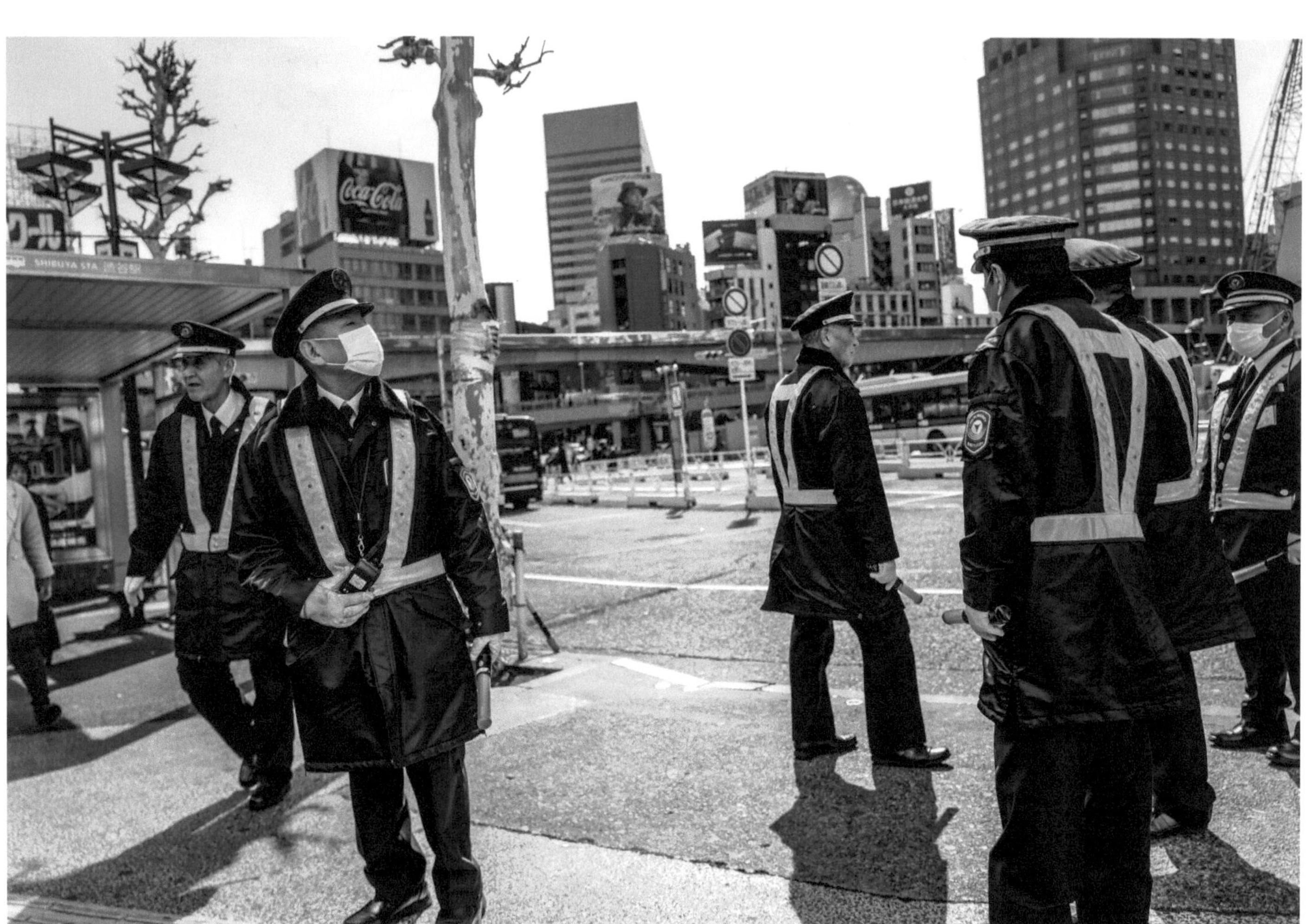
Coca-Cola
SHIBUYA STA.

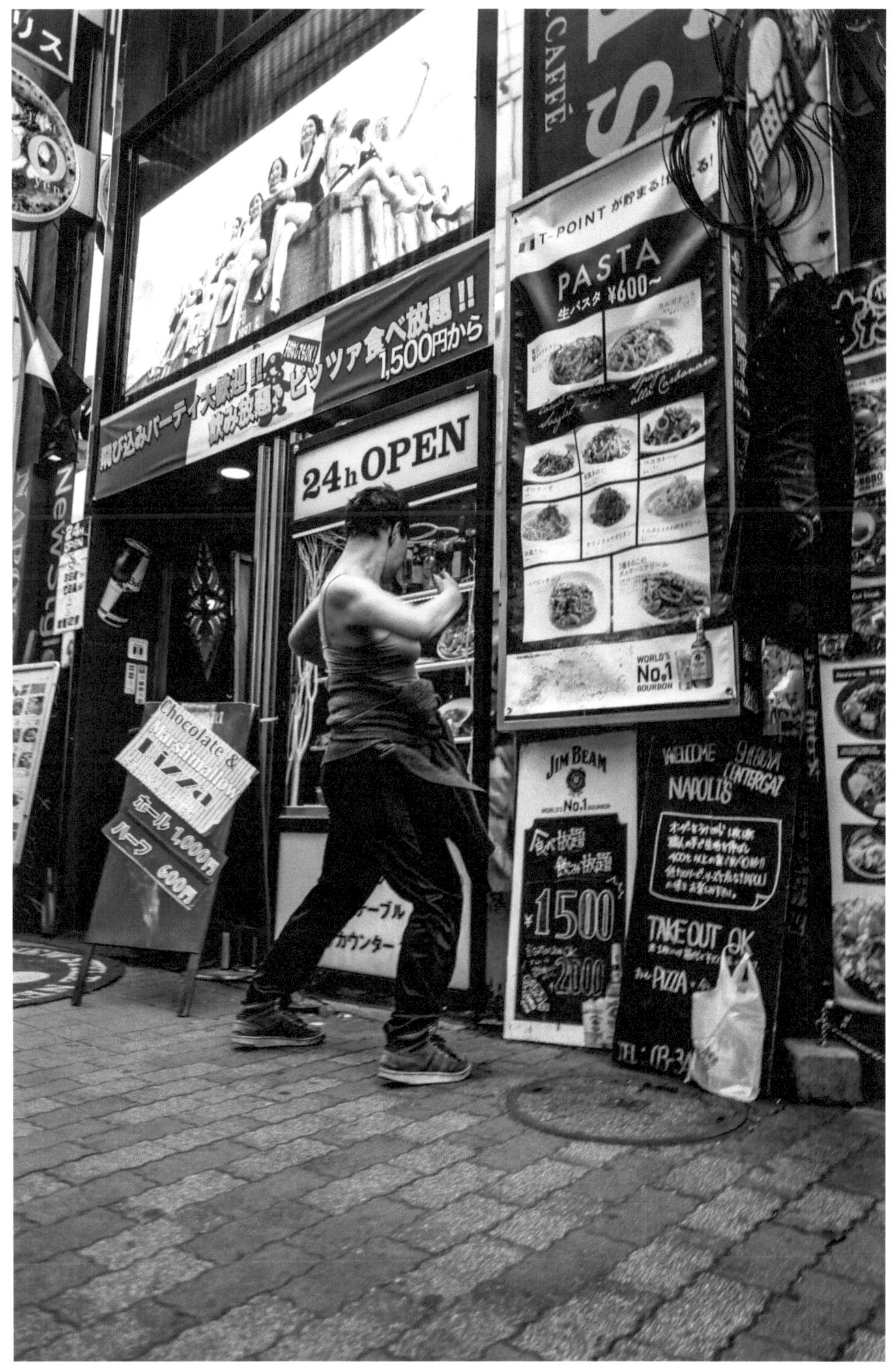

CAFFÈ
T-POINT が貯まる!
PASTA
生パスタ ¥600~
ピッツァ食べ放題!!
1,500円から
飲み放題
24hOPEN
Chocolate &
Marshmallow
ホール 1,000円
ハーフ 600円
JIM BEAM
No.1
食べ放題
飲み放題
1500
WORLD'S
No.1
BOURBON
WELCOME
NAPOLI'S
TAKE OUT OK
PIZZA

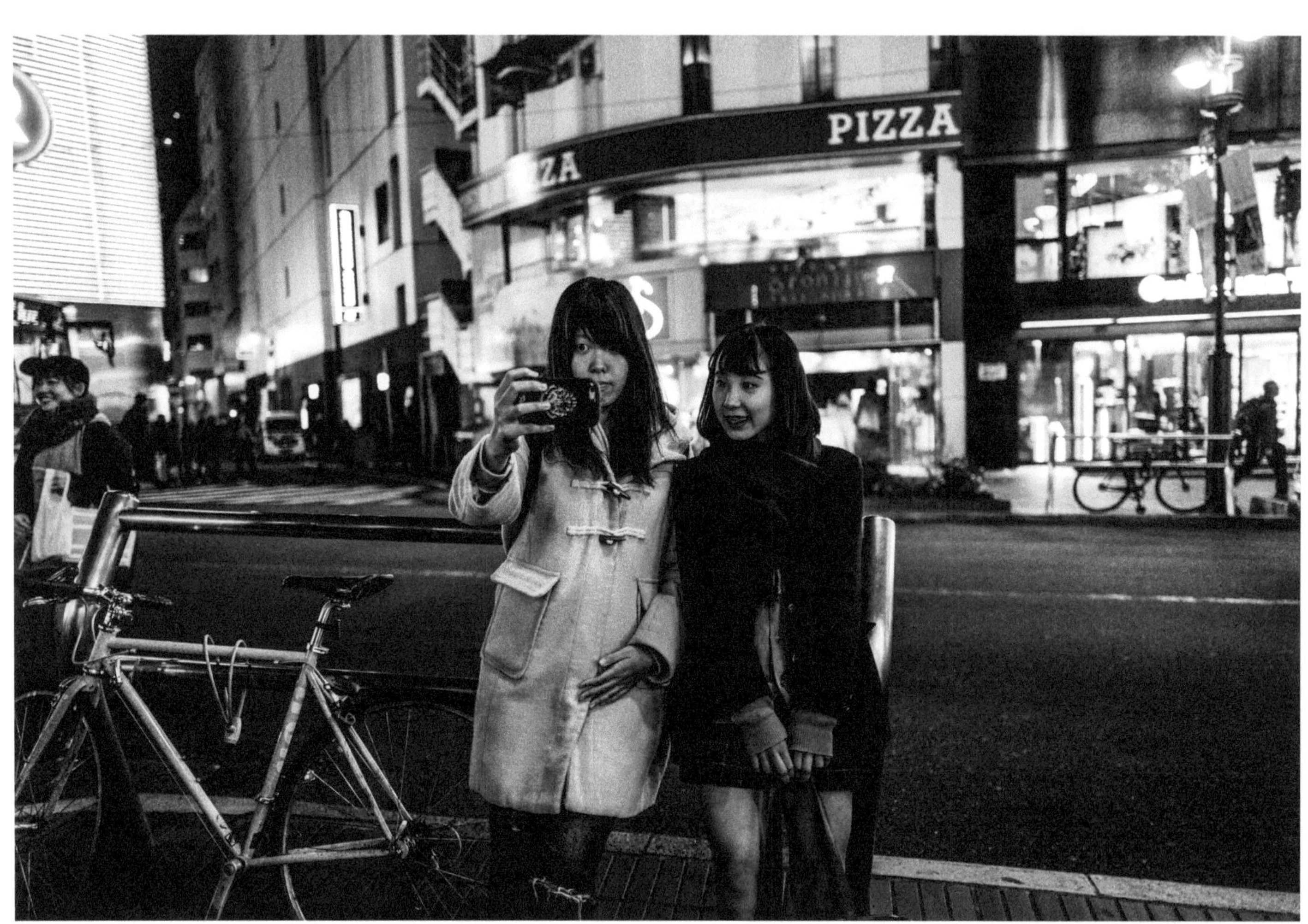
PIZZA

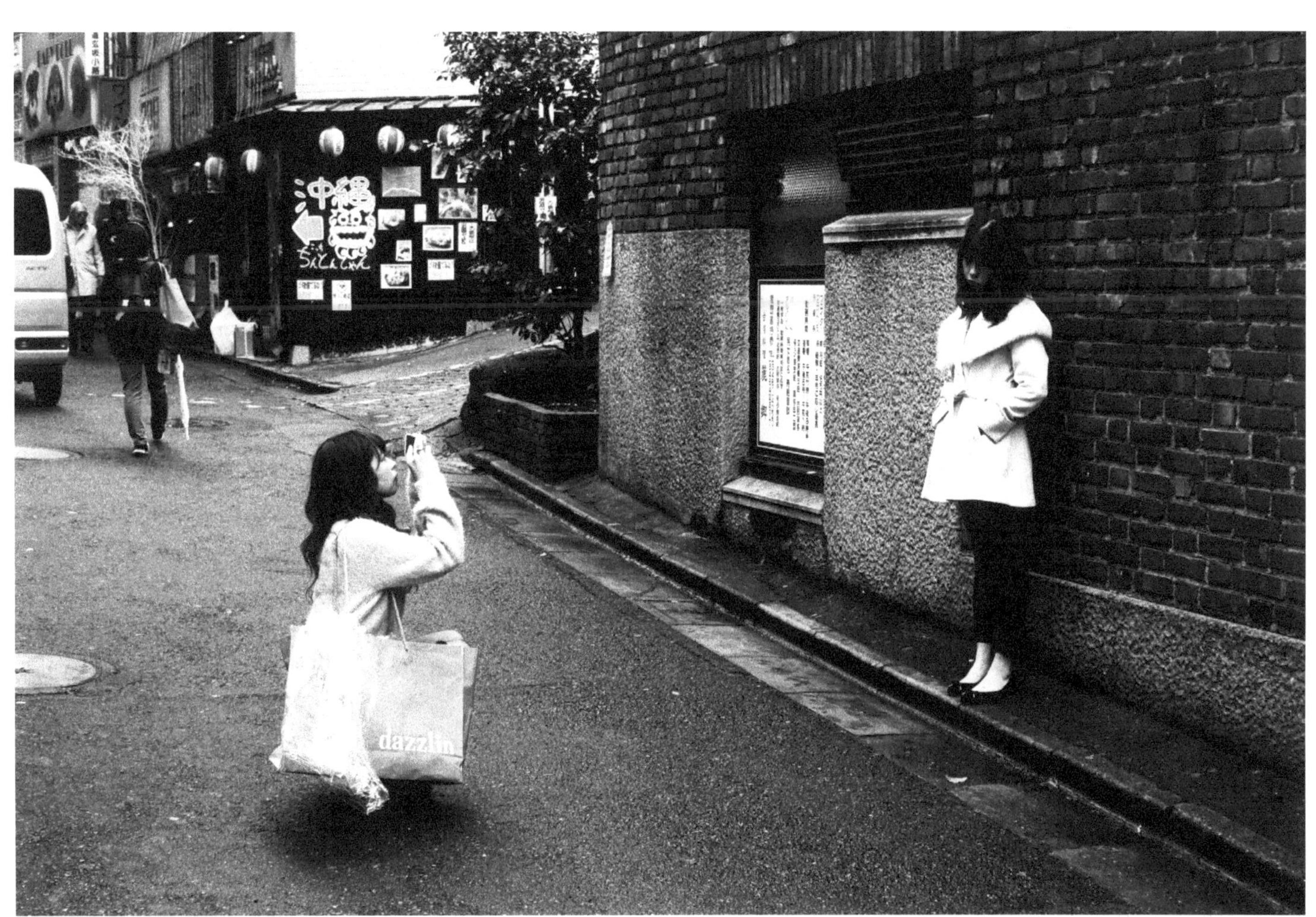
沖縄
dazzlin

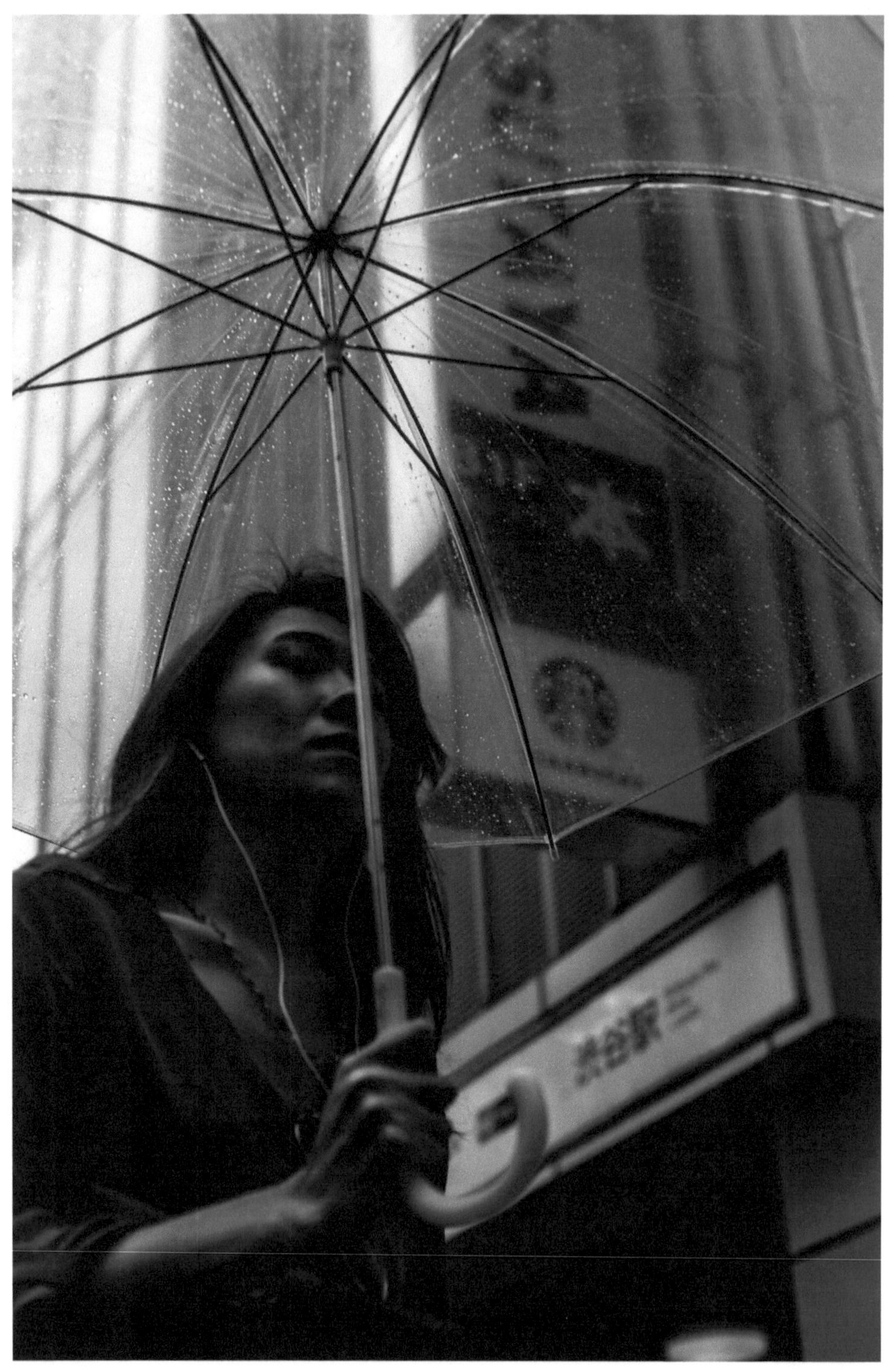
渋谷駅

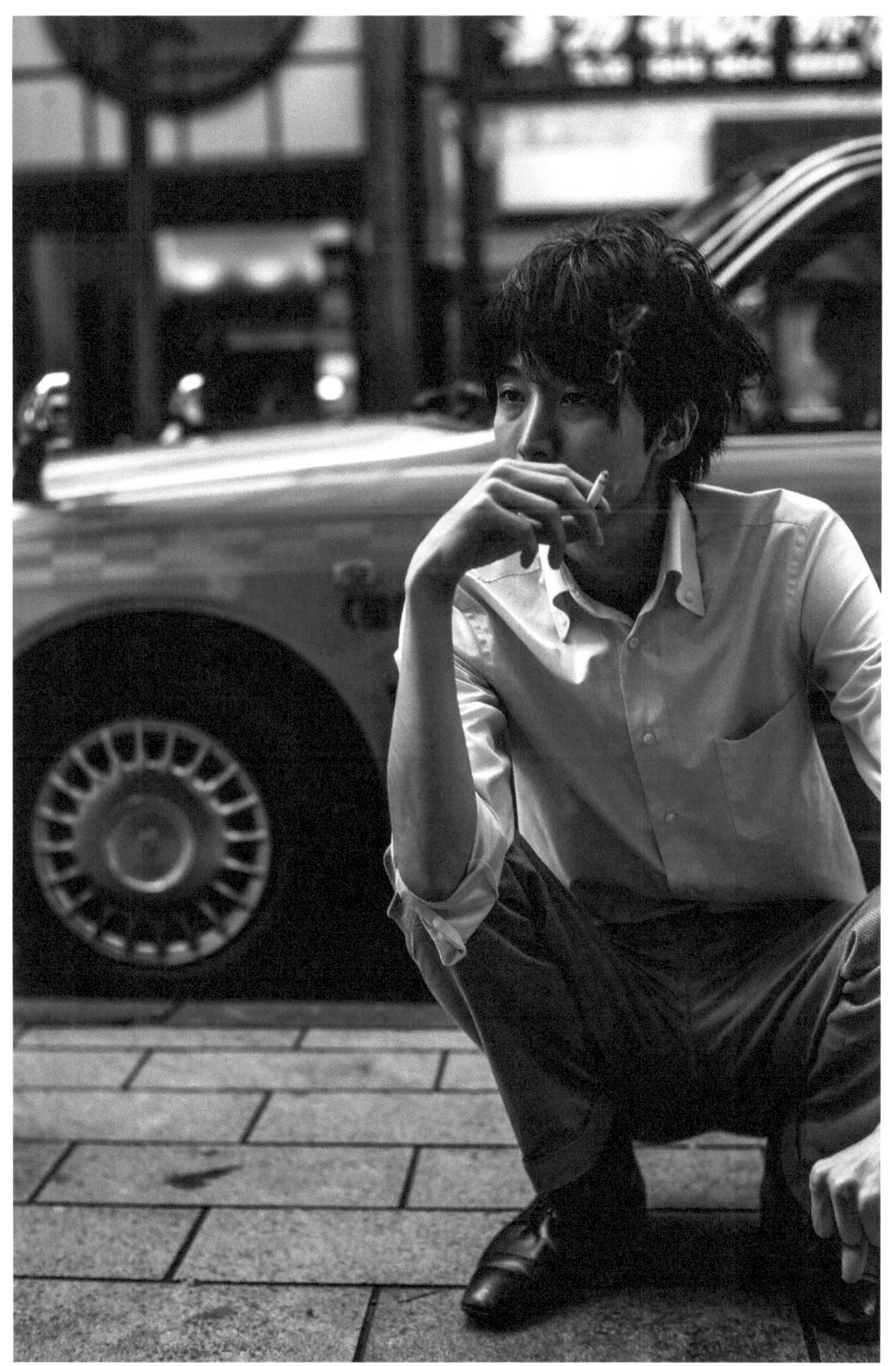

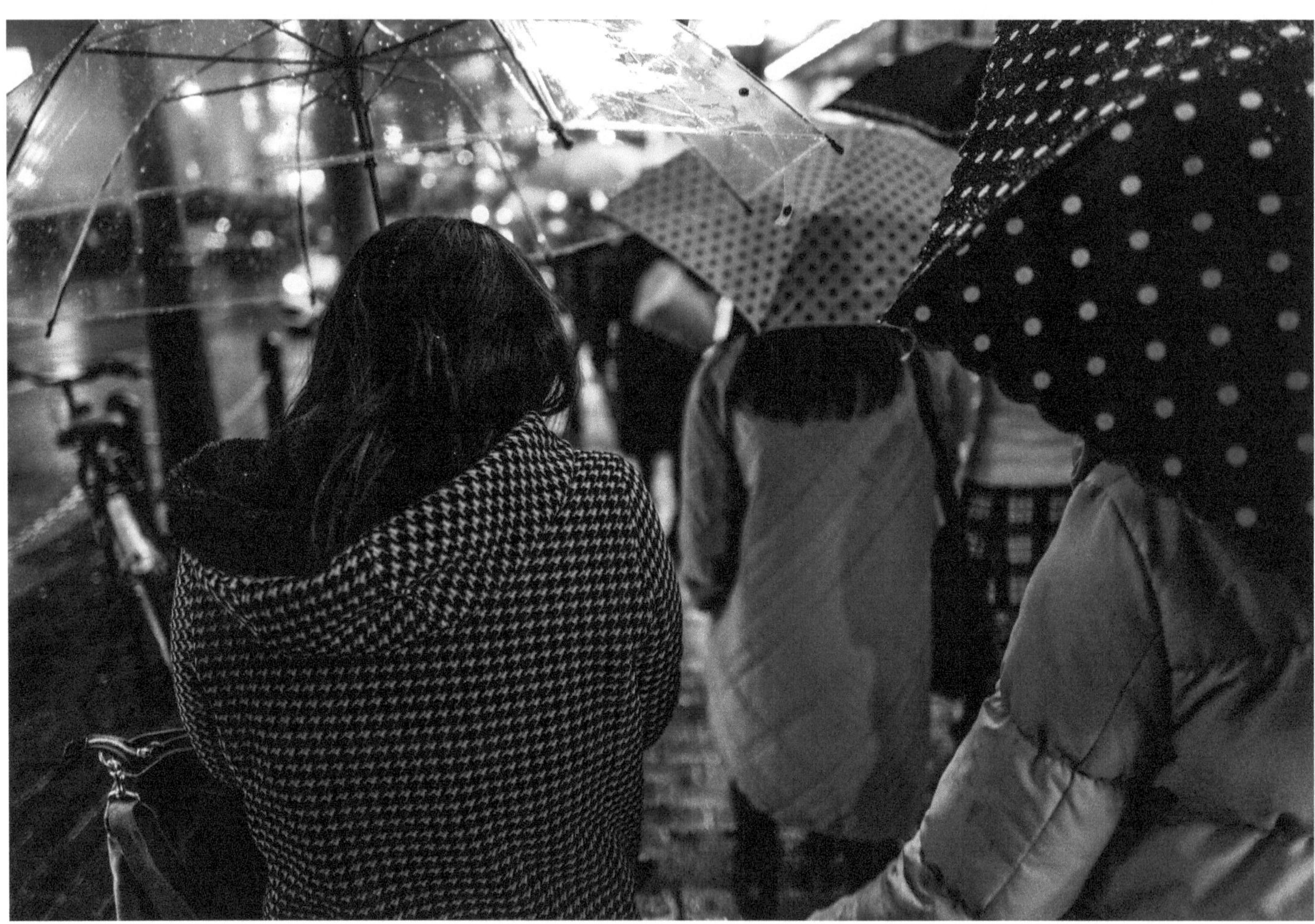

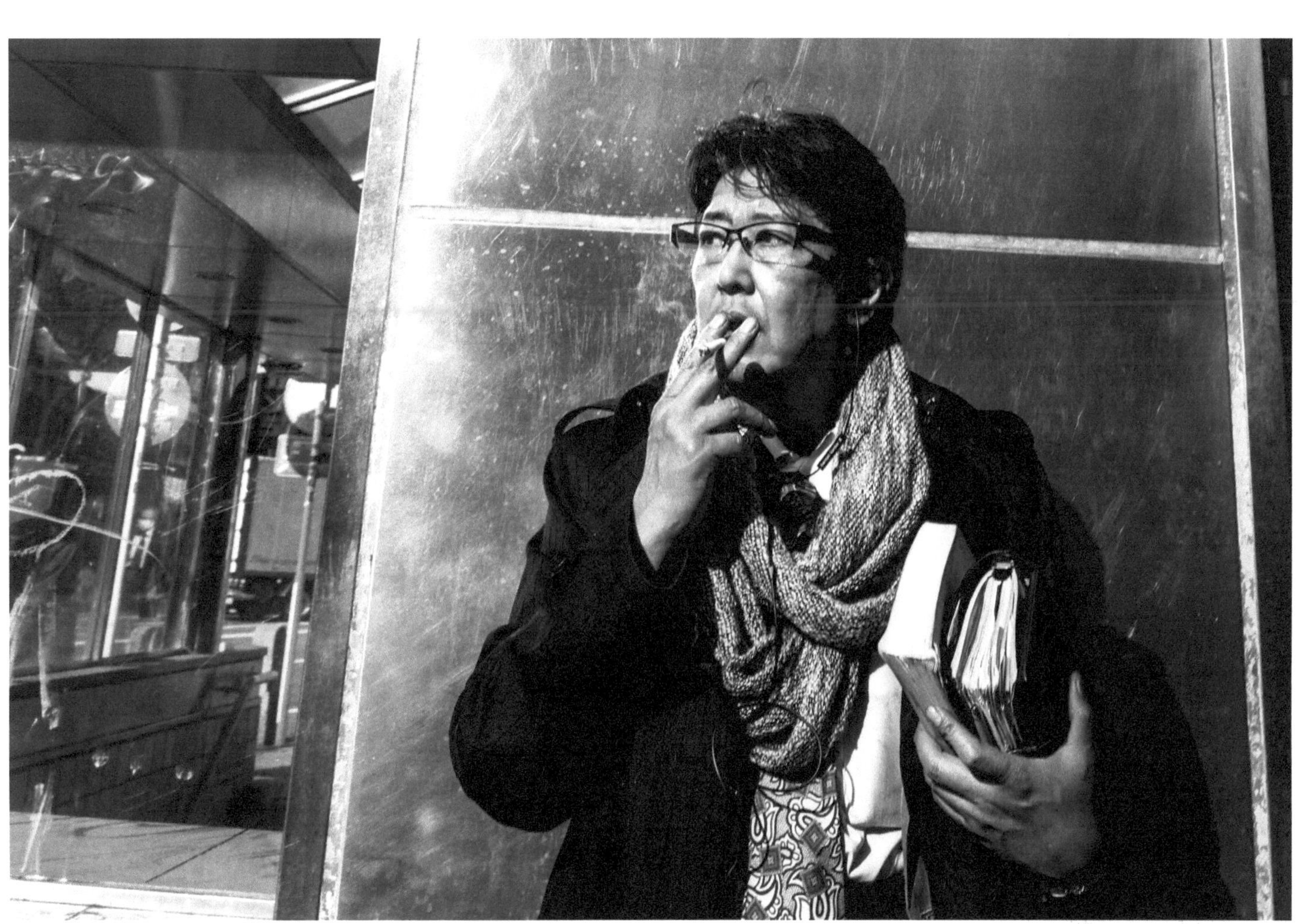

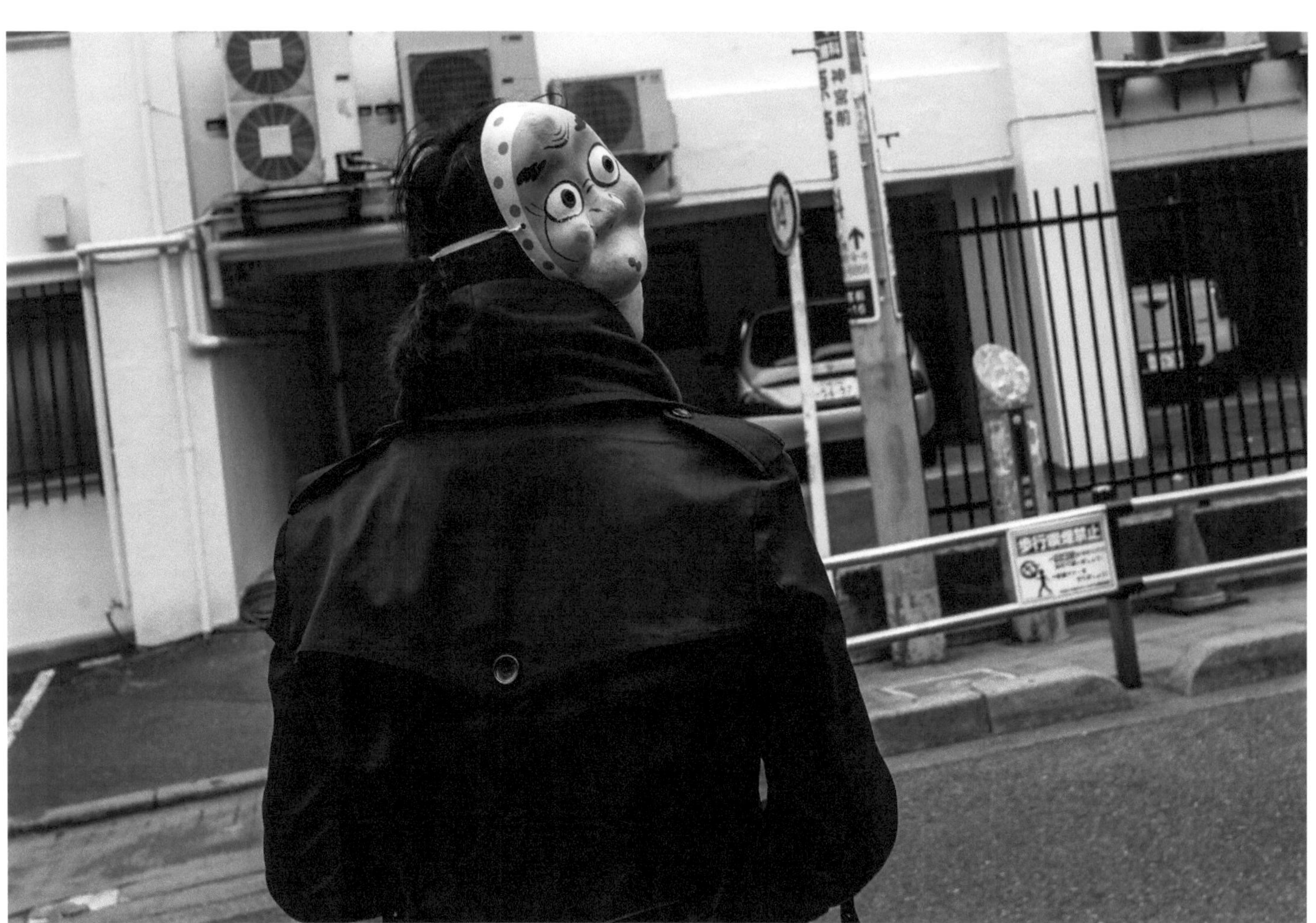
神宮前
歩行喫煙禁止

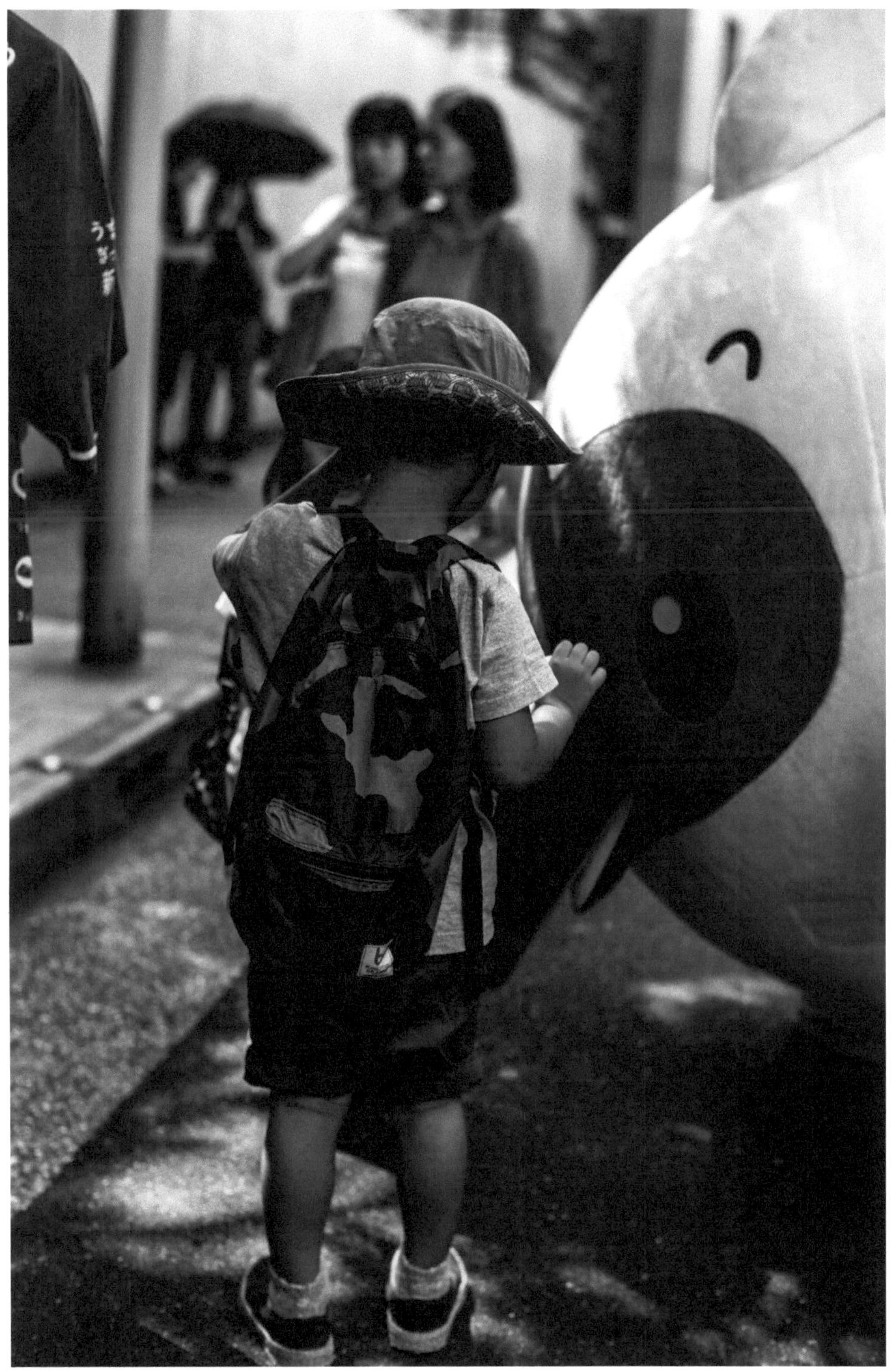

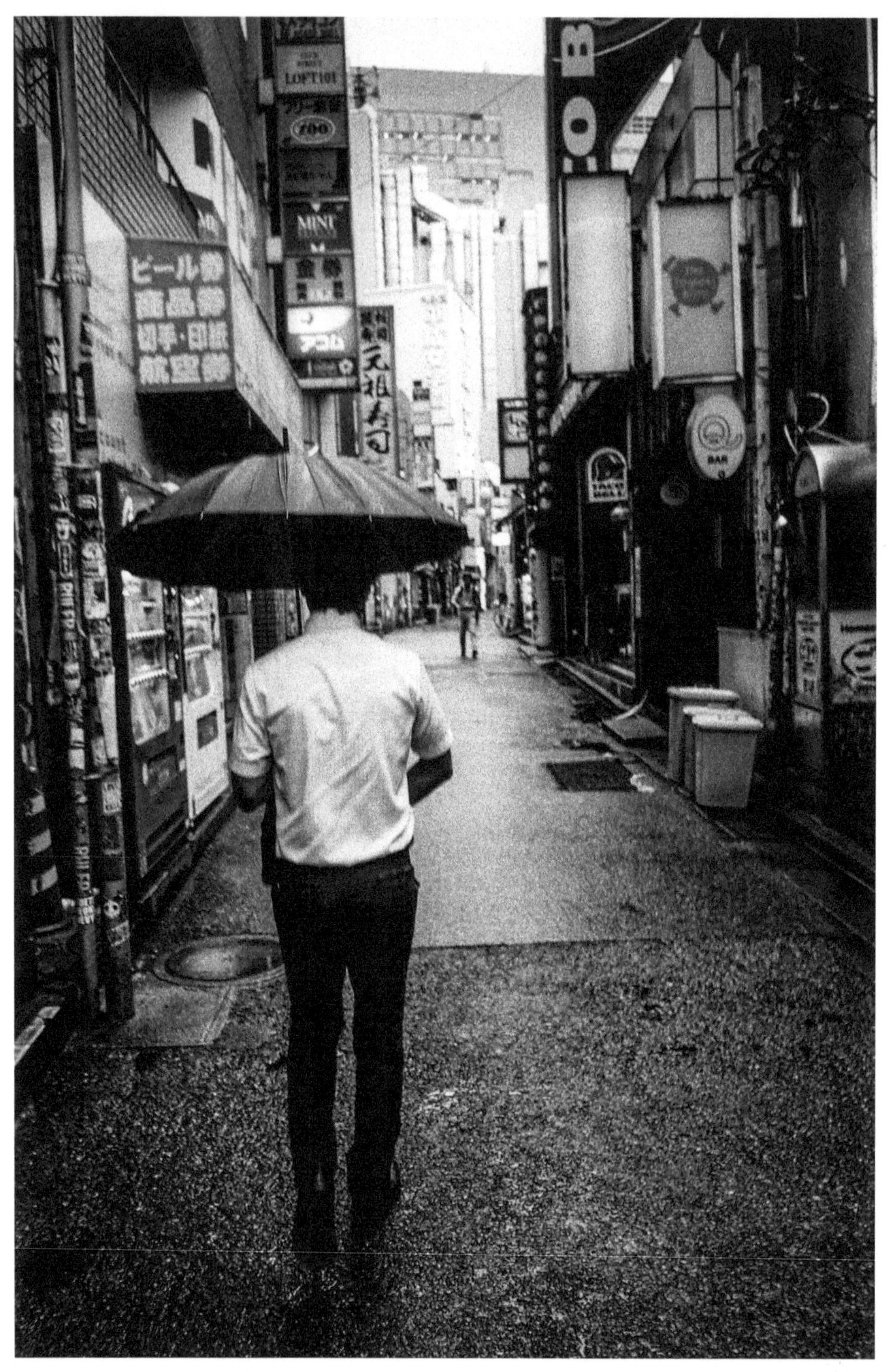
ビール券
アコム
元祖寿司
BAR

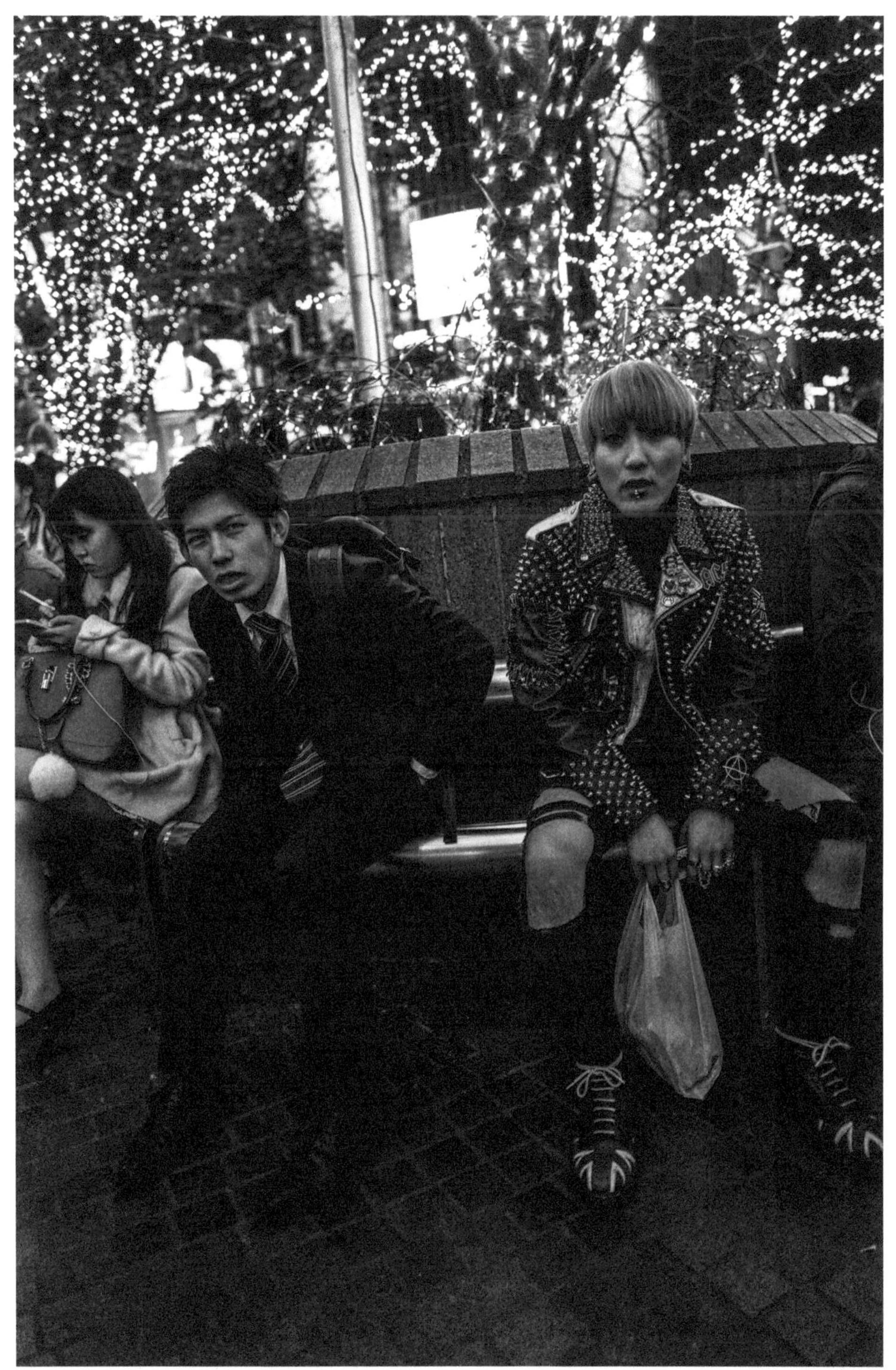

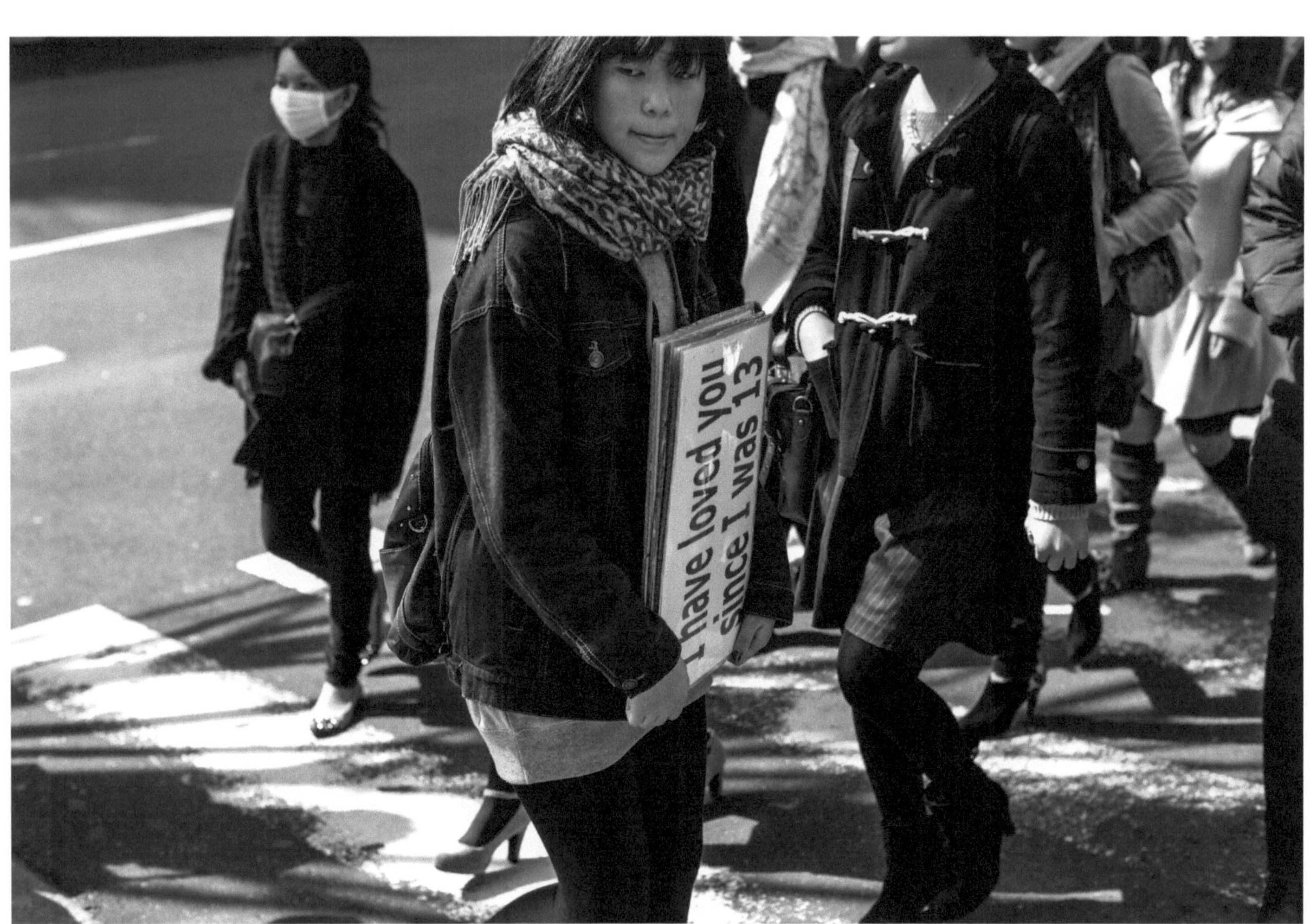
I have loved you
since I was 13

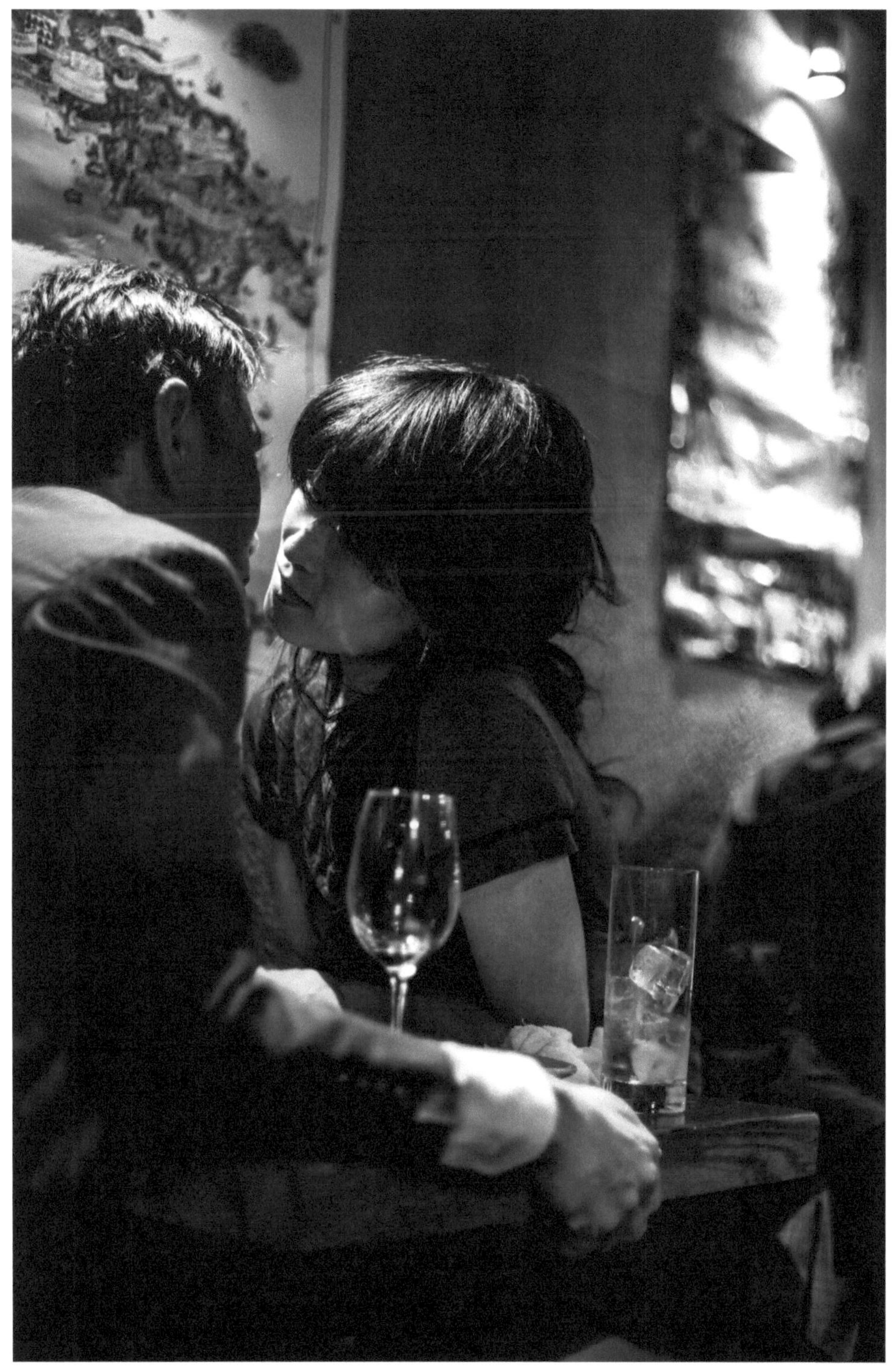

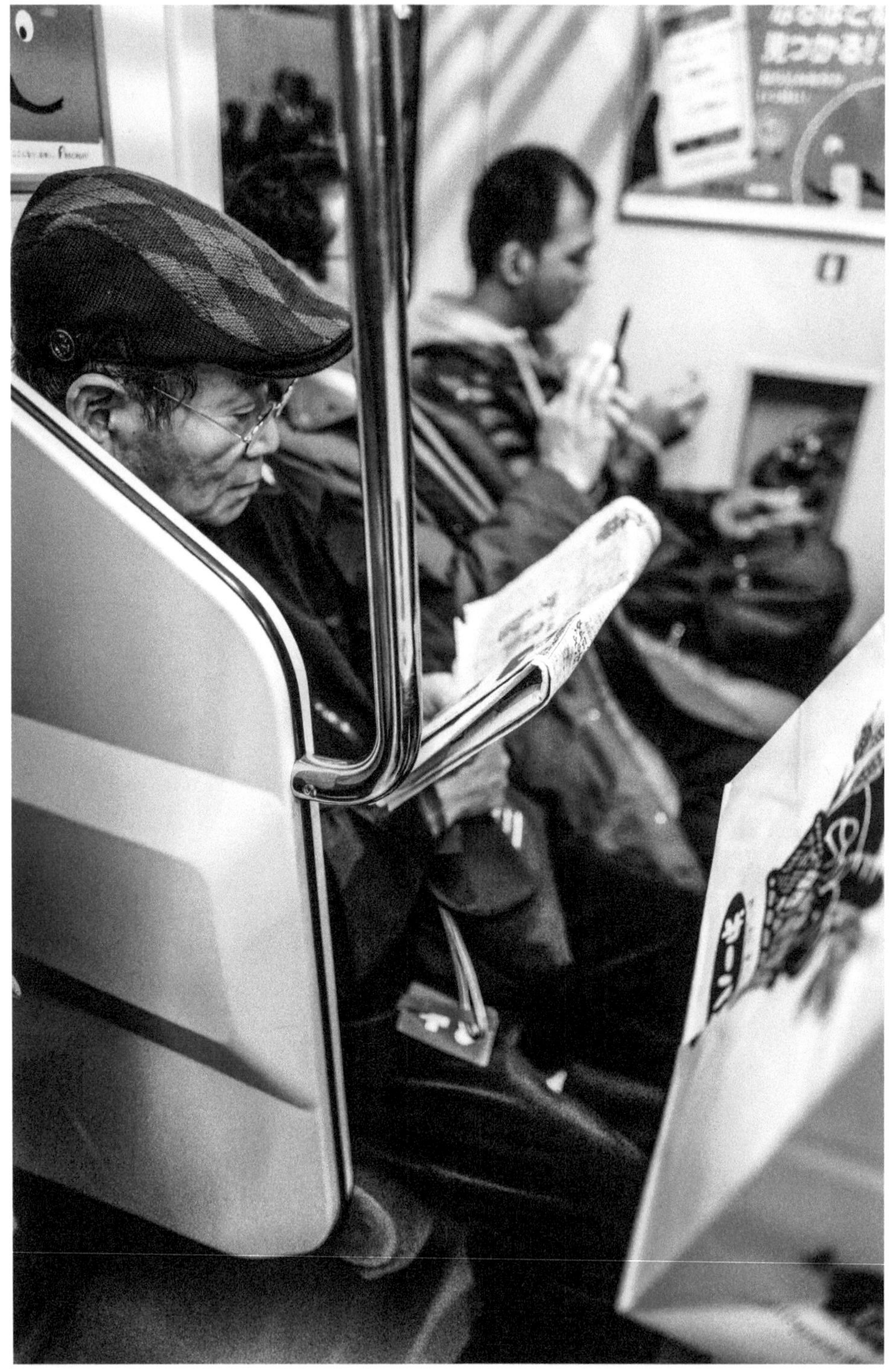

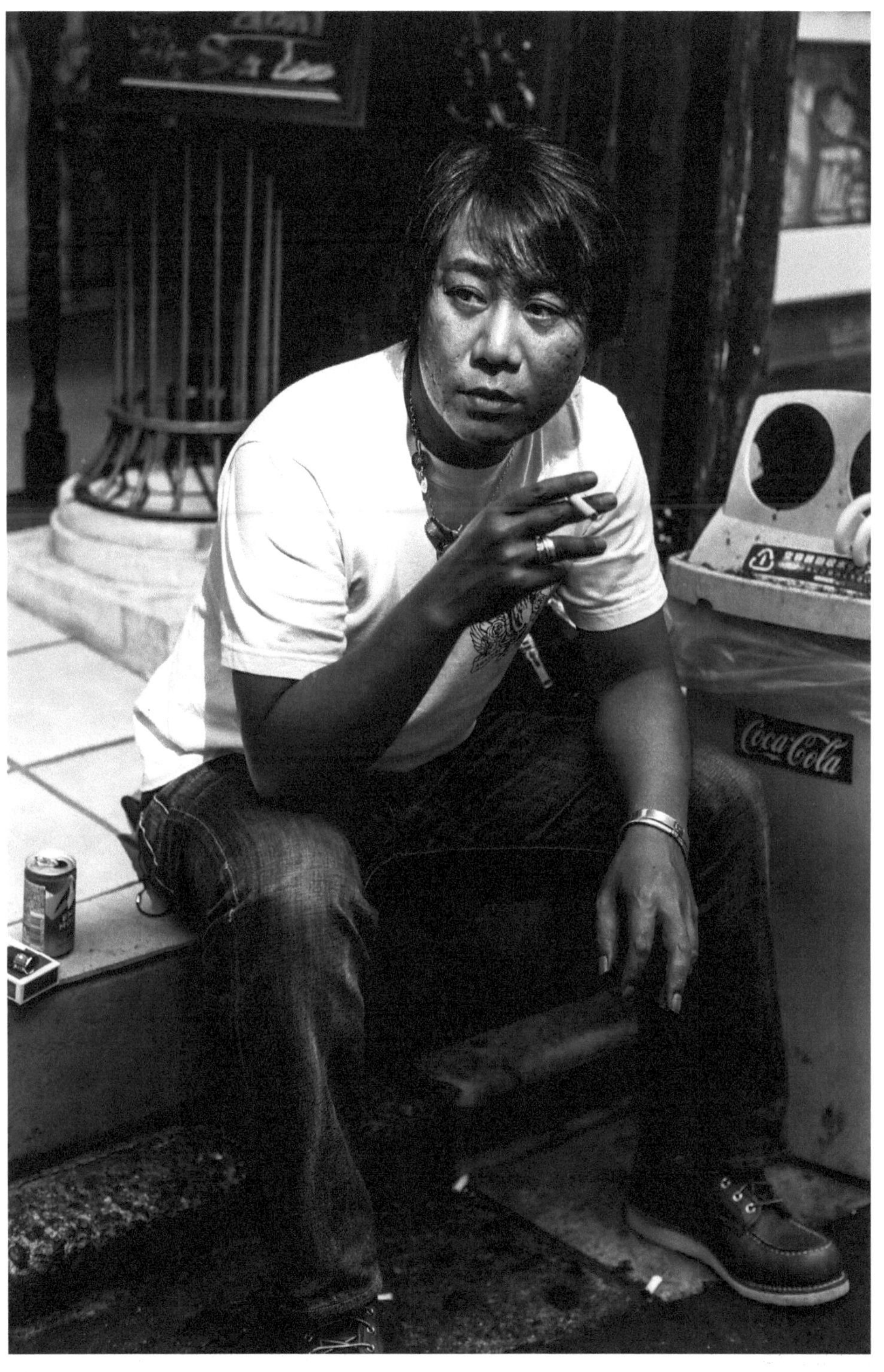
Coca-Cola

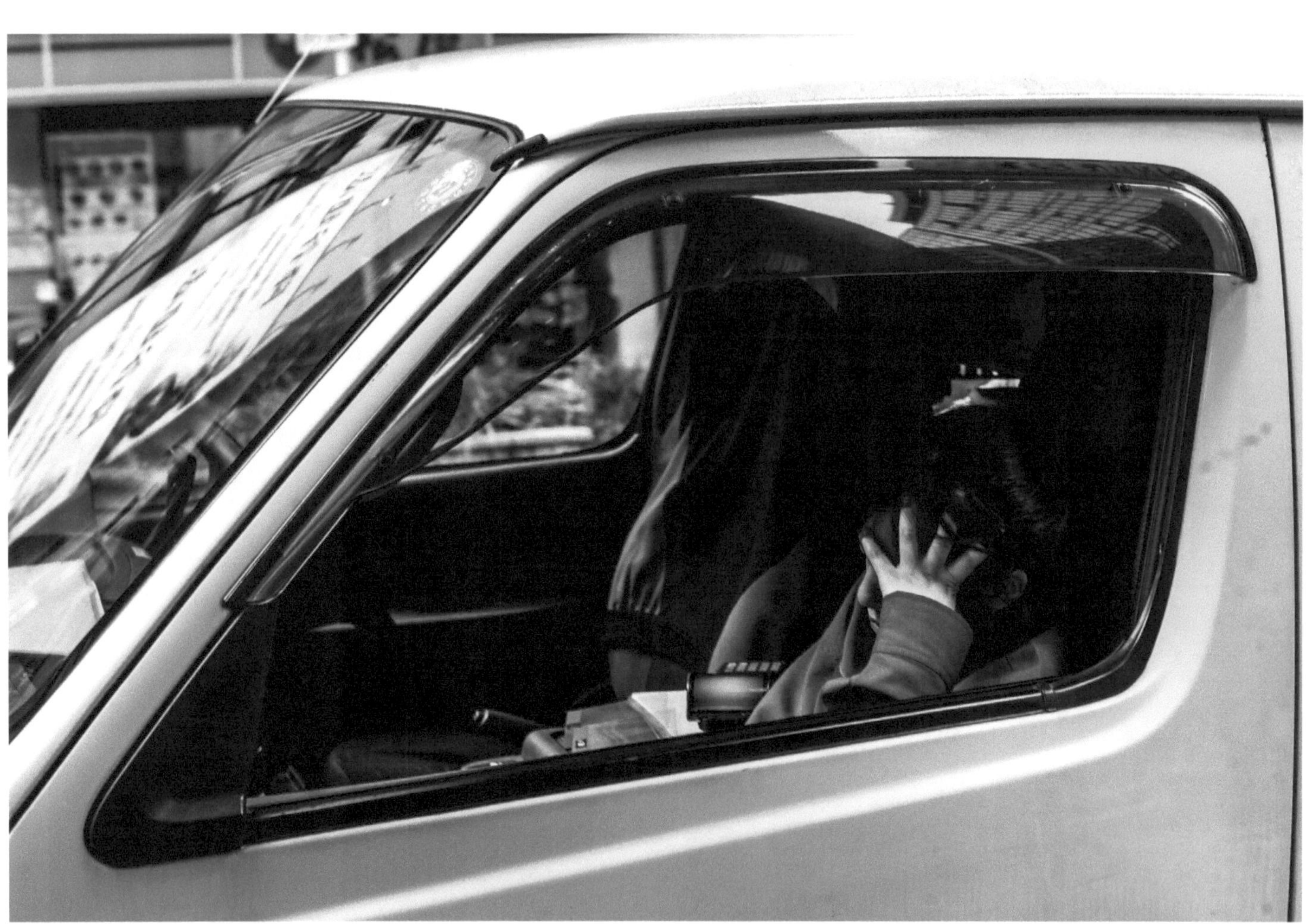

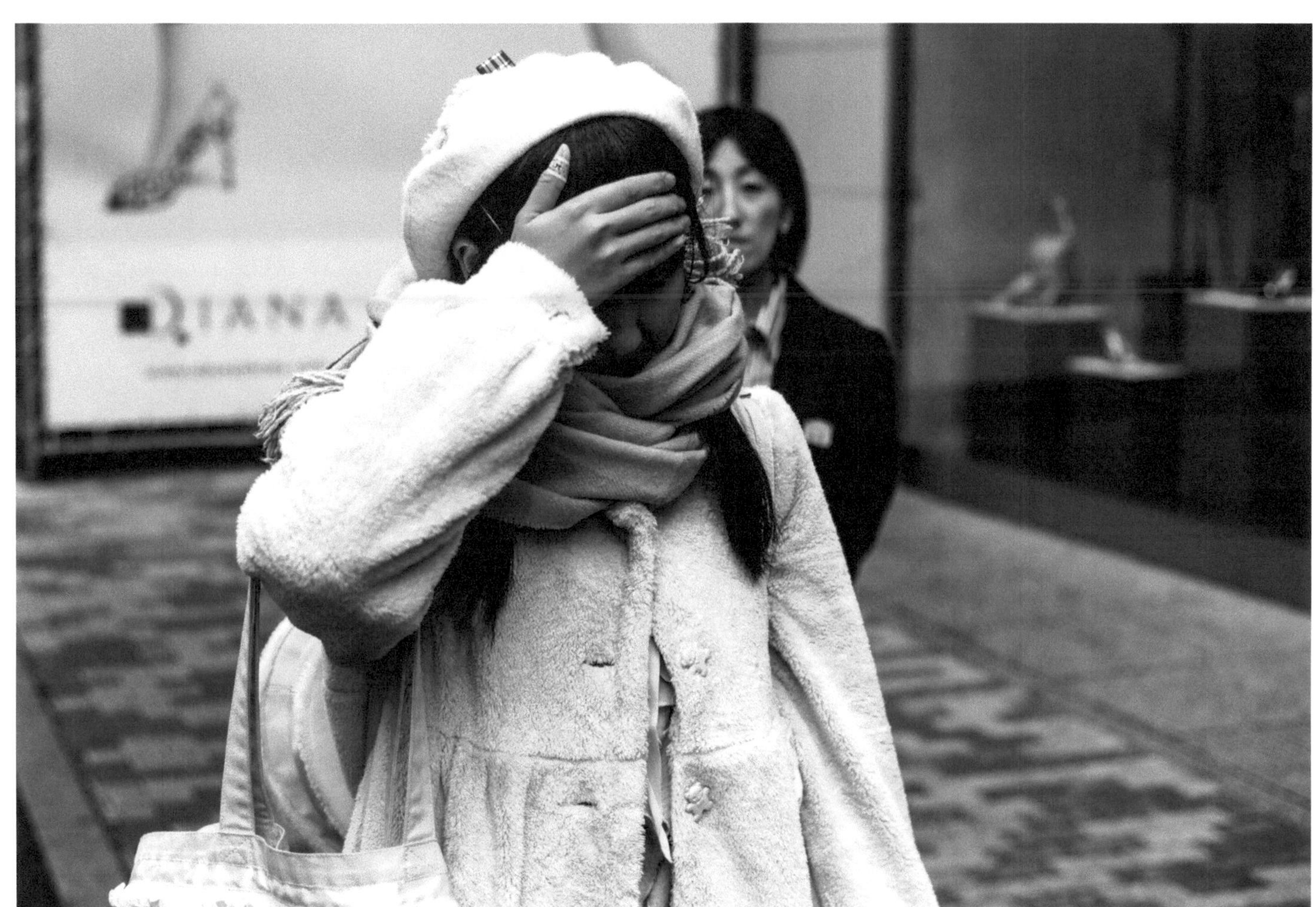

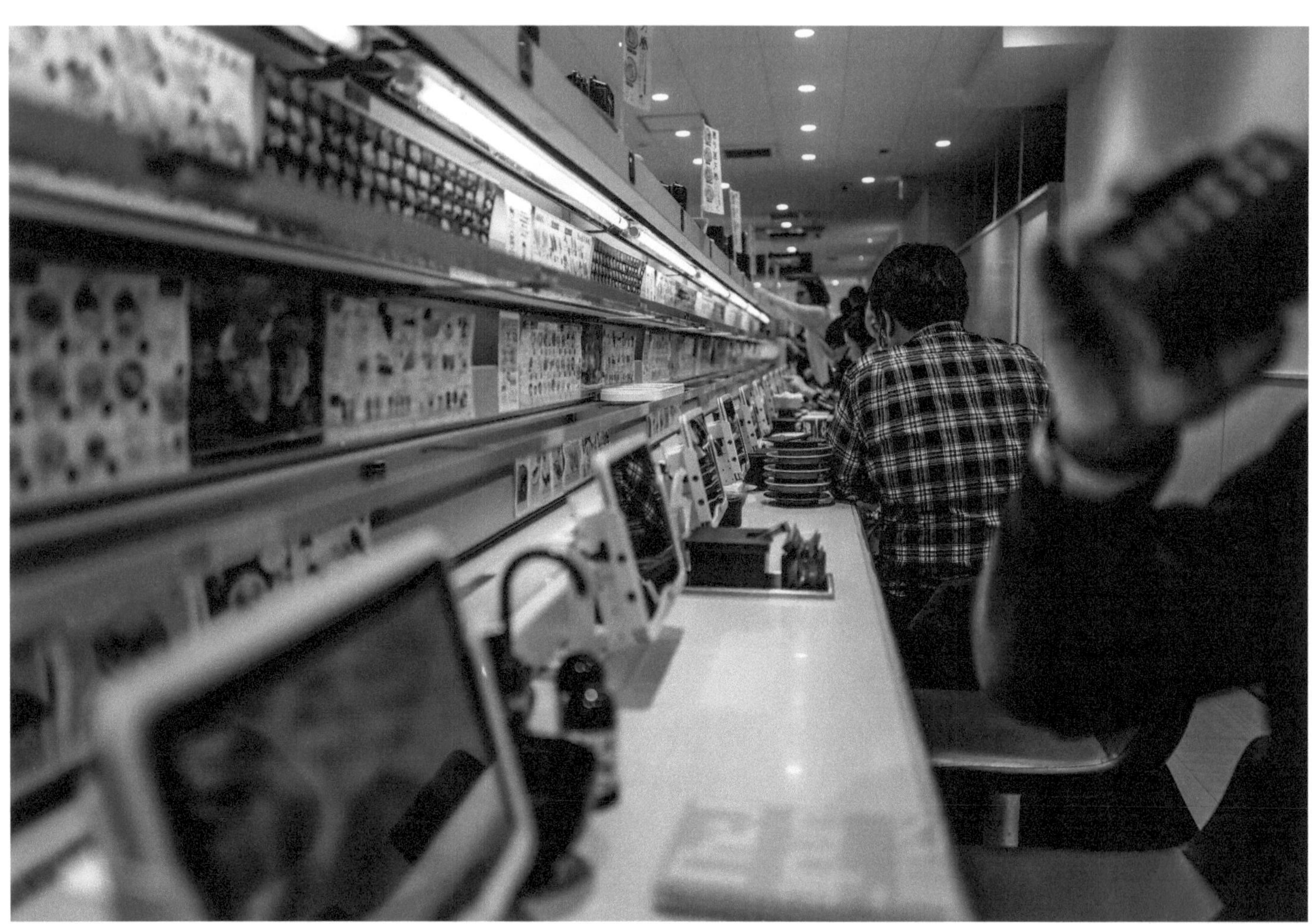

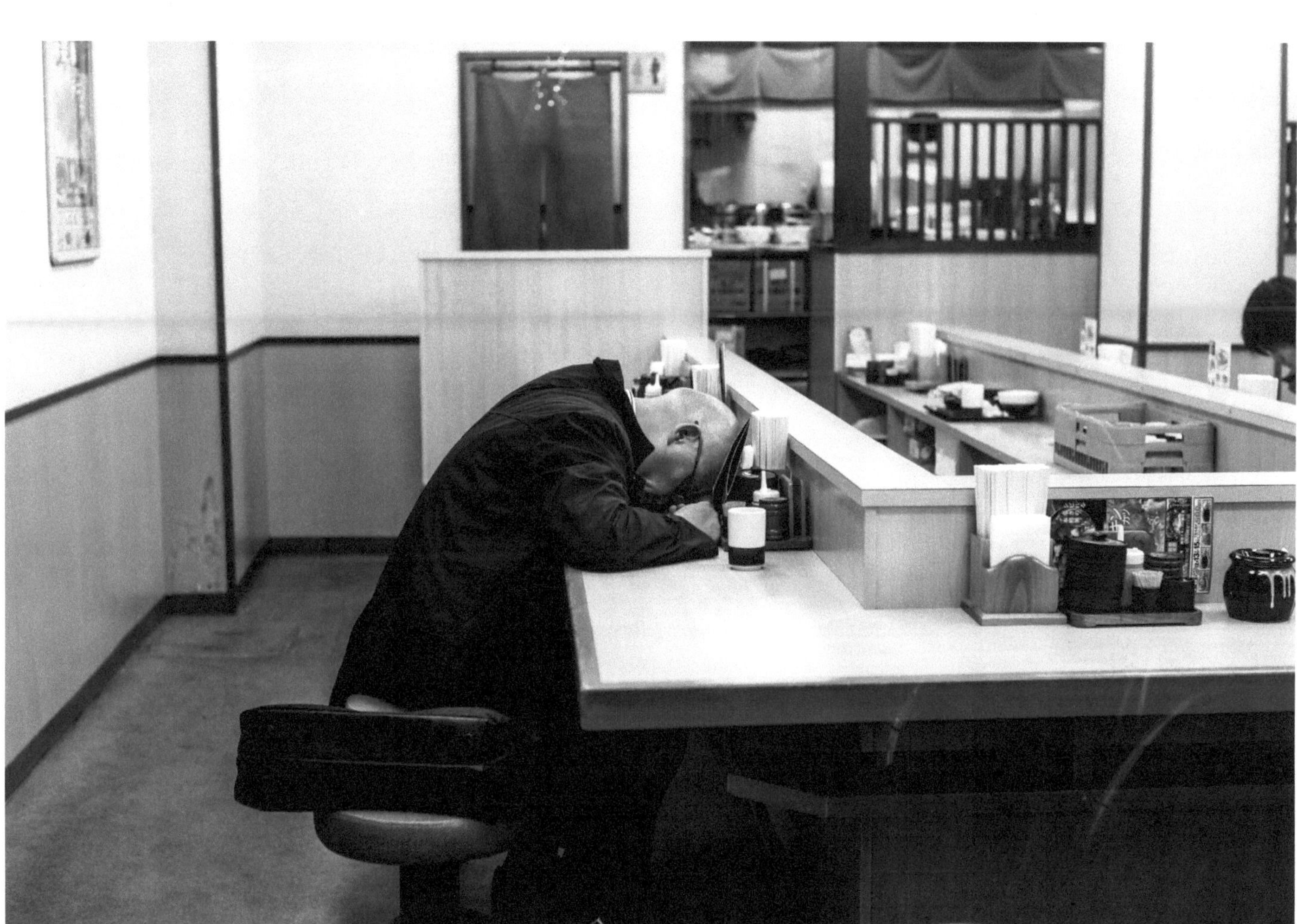

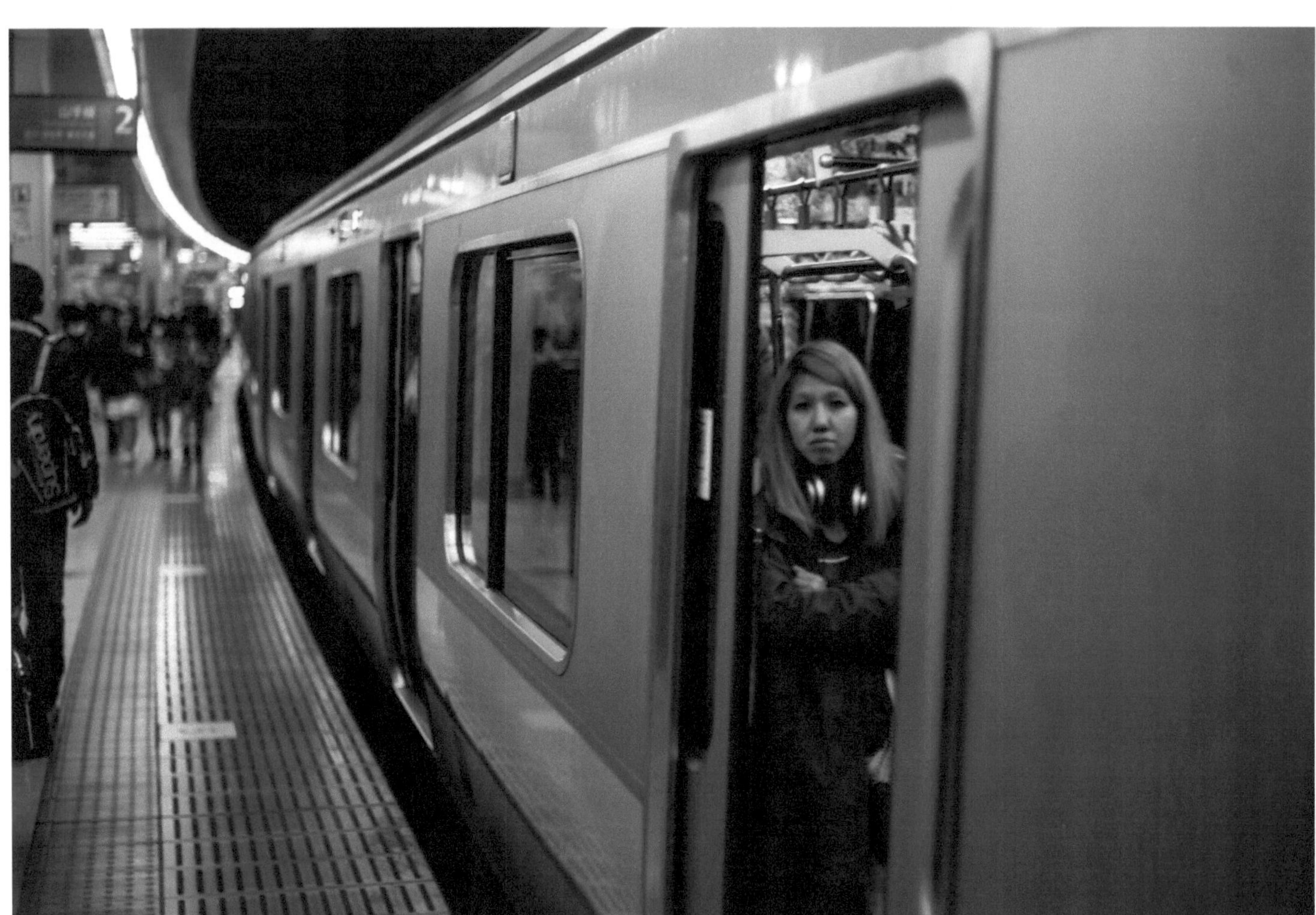

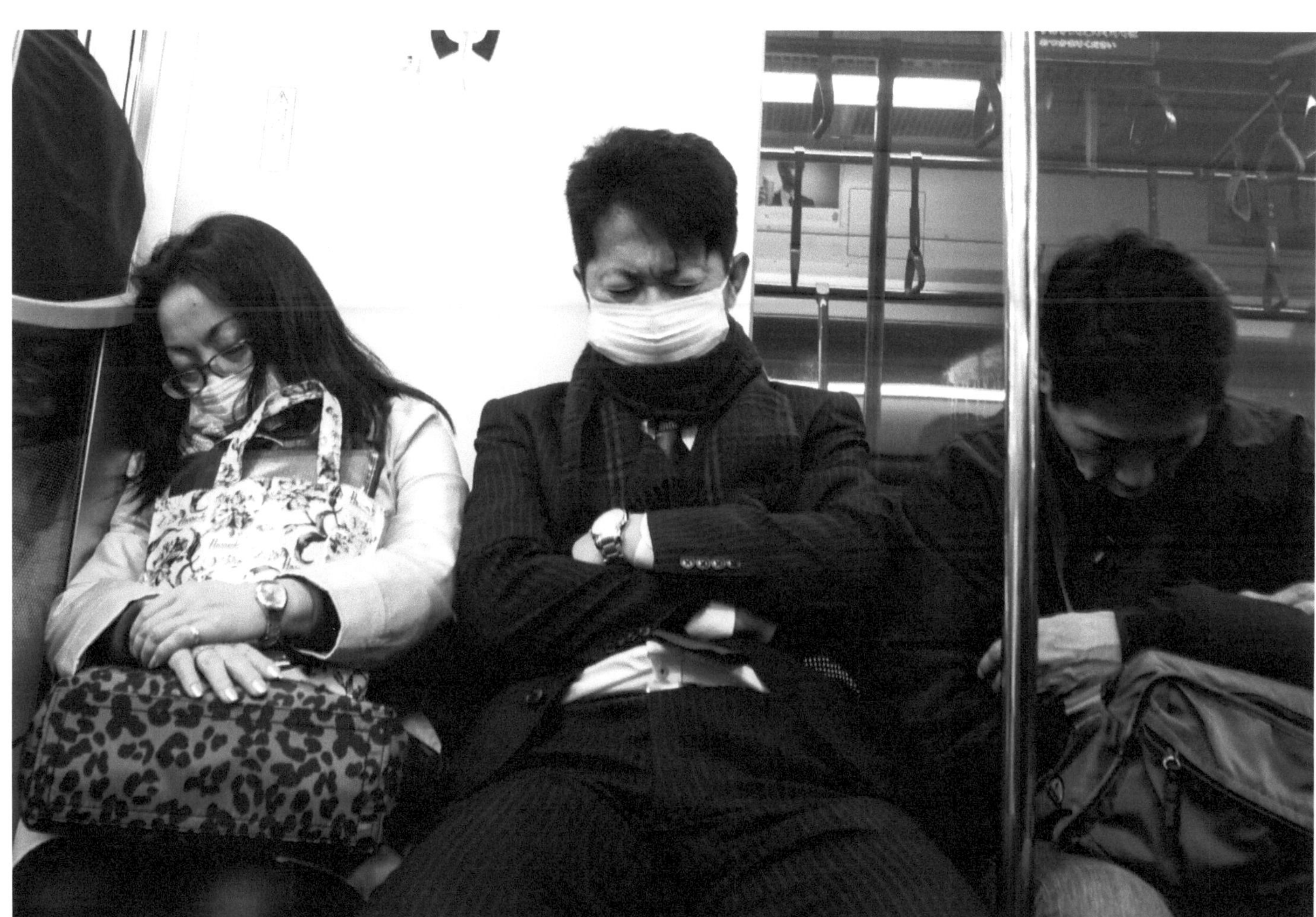

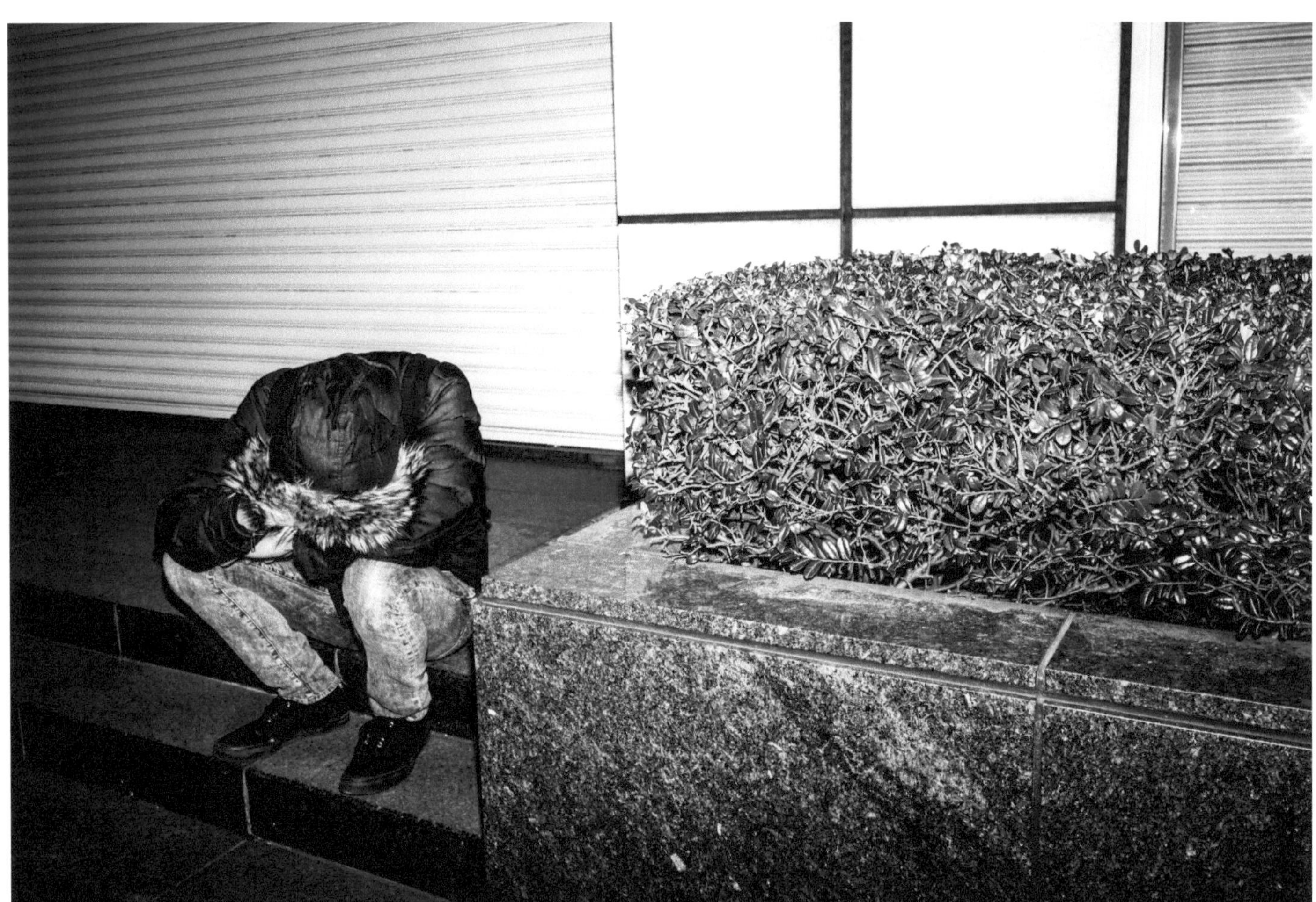

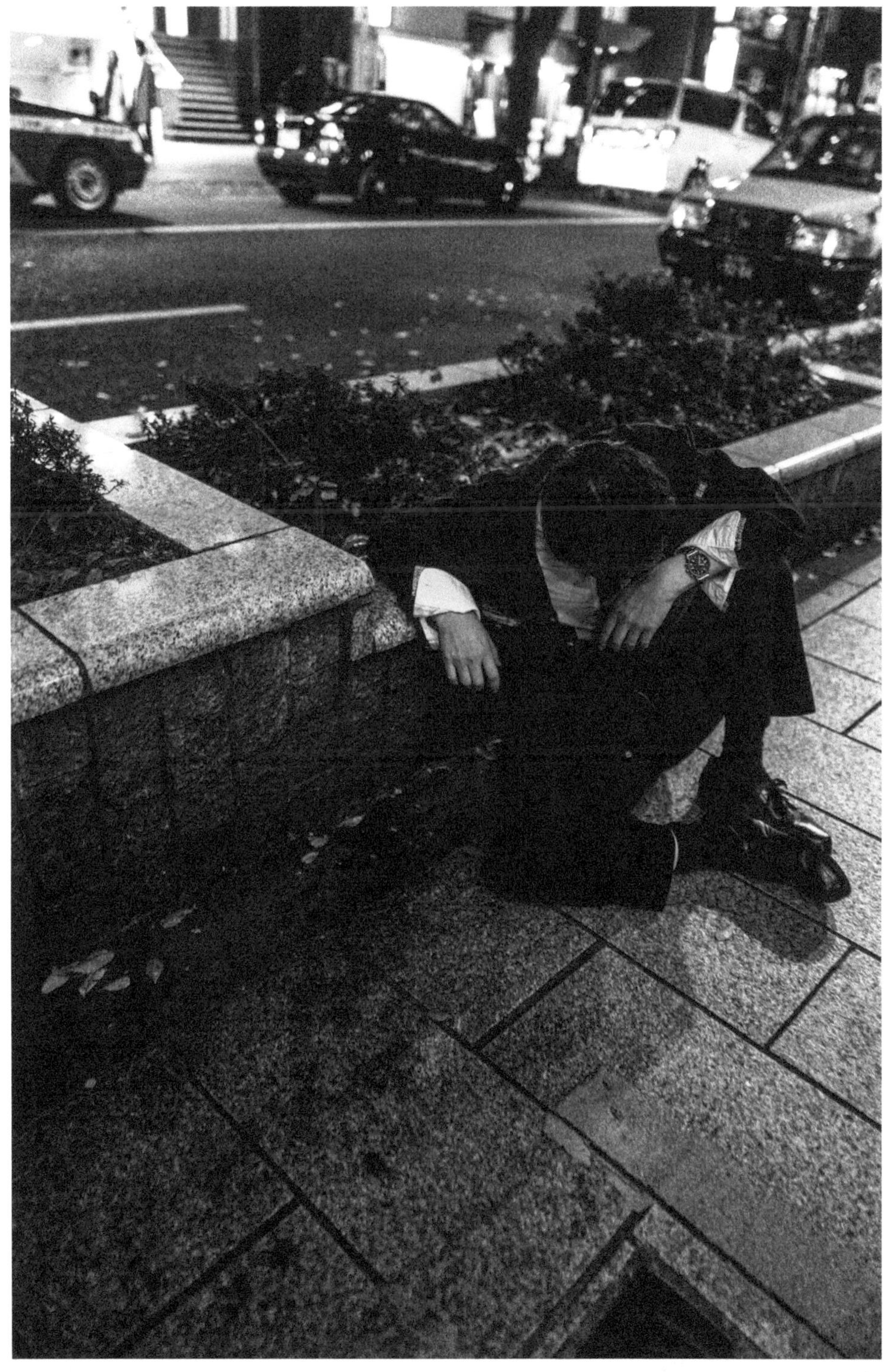

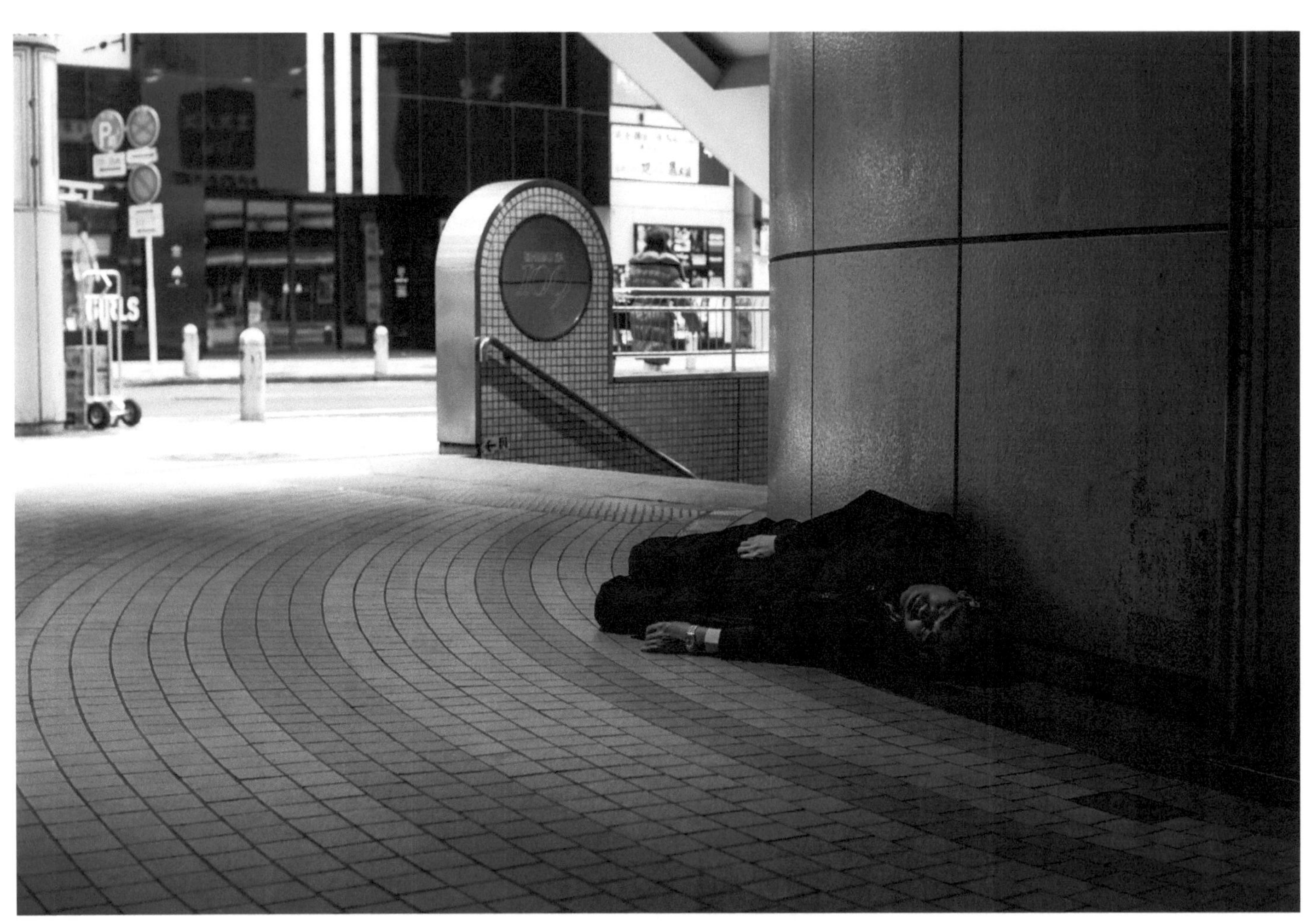

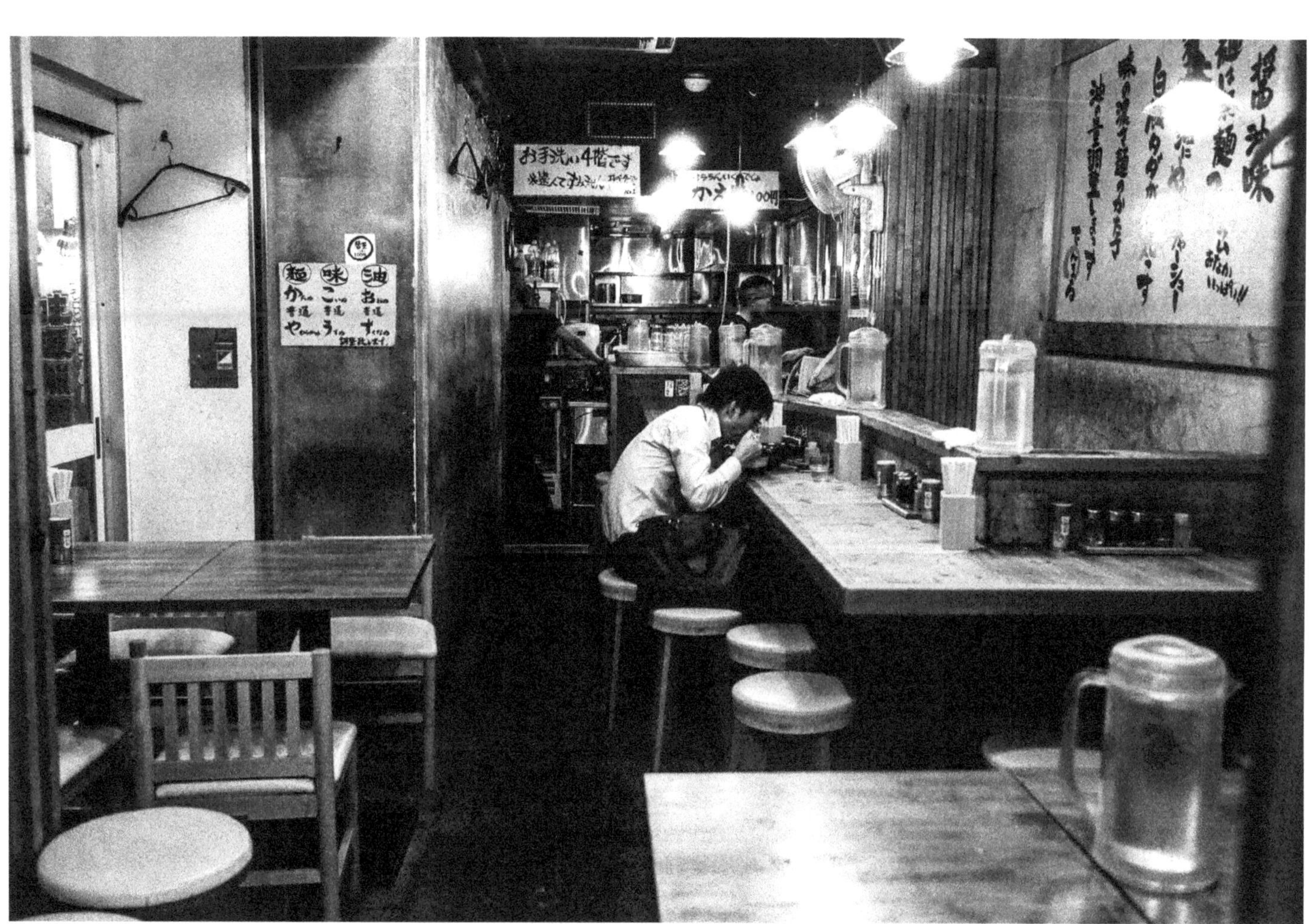
お手洗い4階です

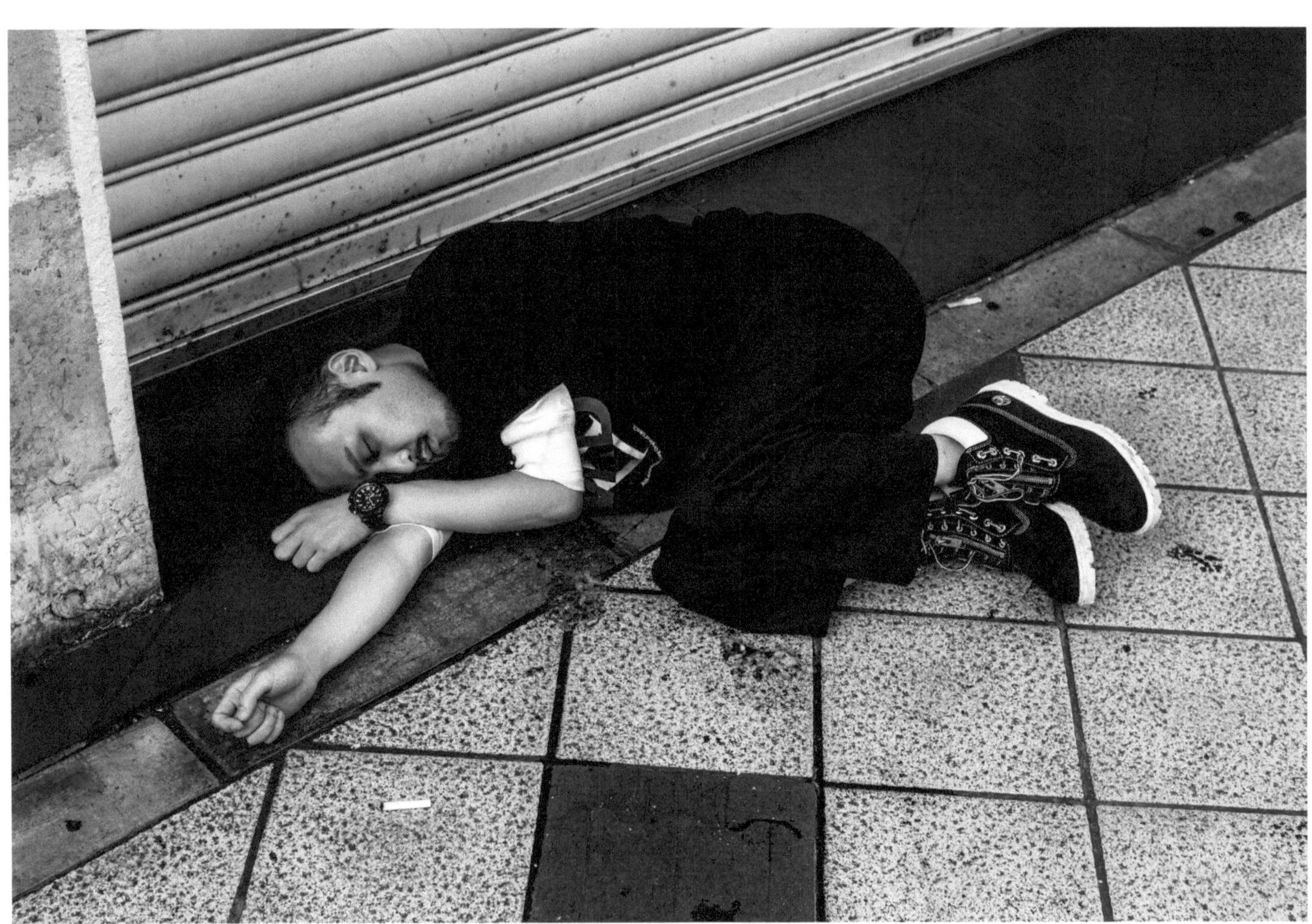

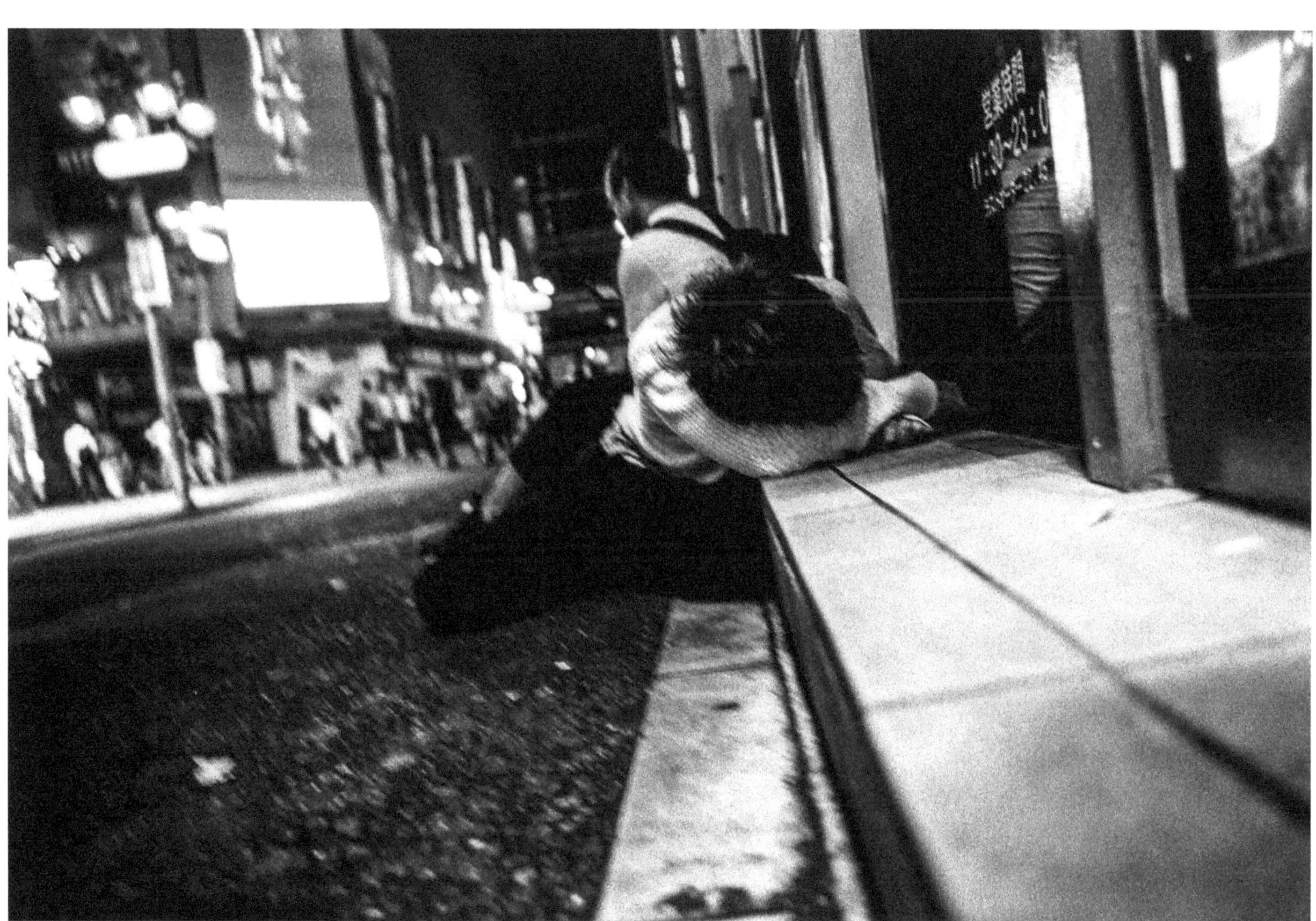
営業時間
11:00~23:0

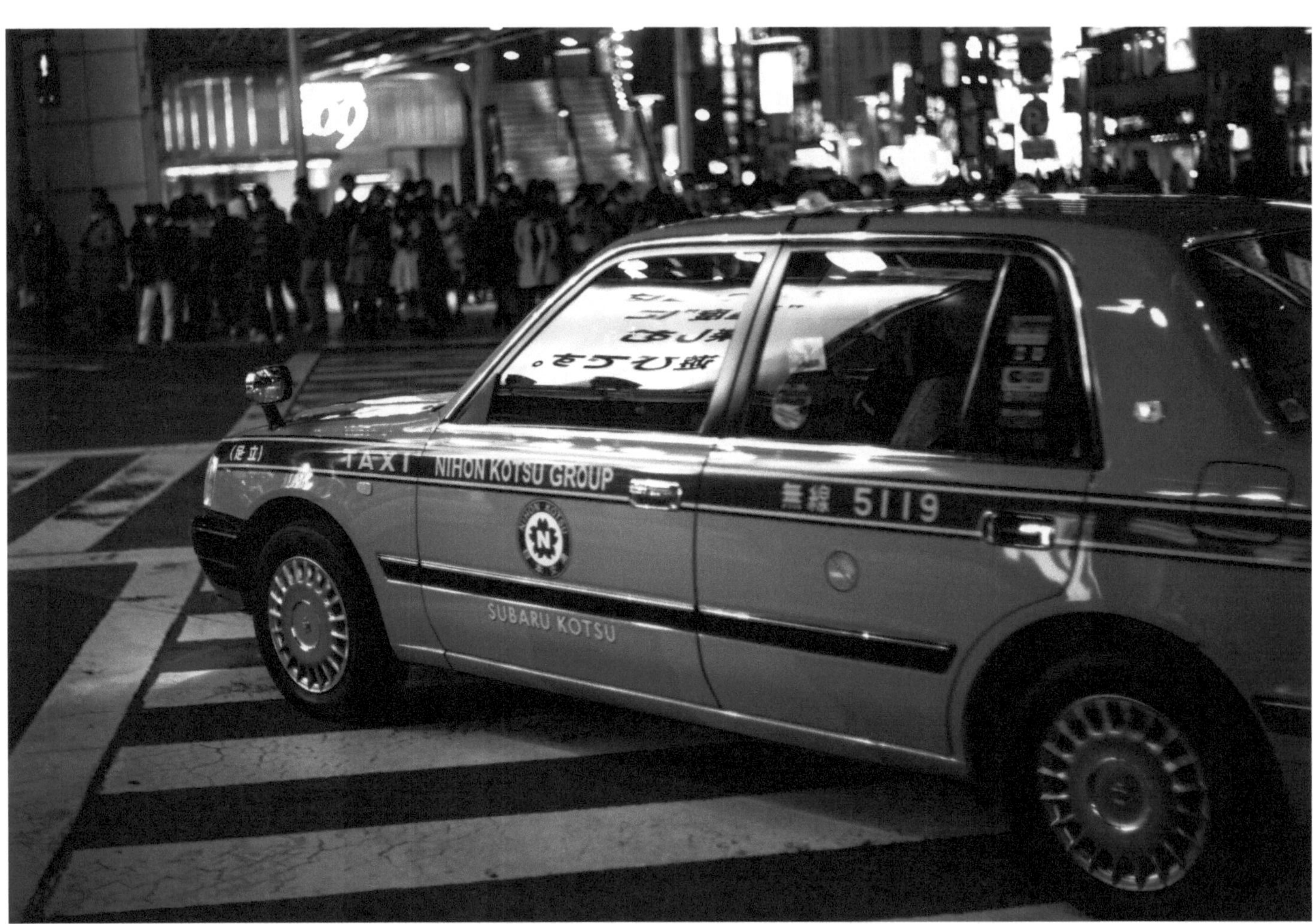
(足立)
TAXI
NIHON KOTSU GROUP
無線 5119
SUBARU KOTSU

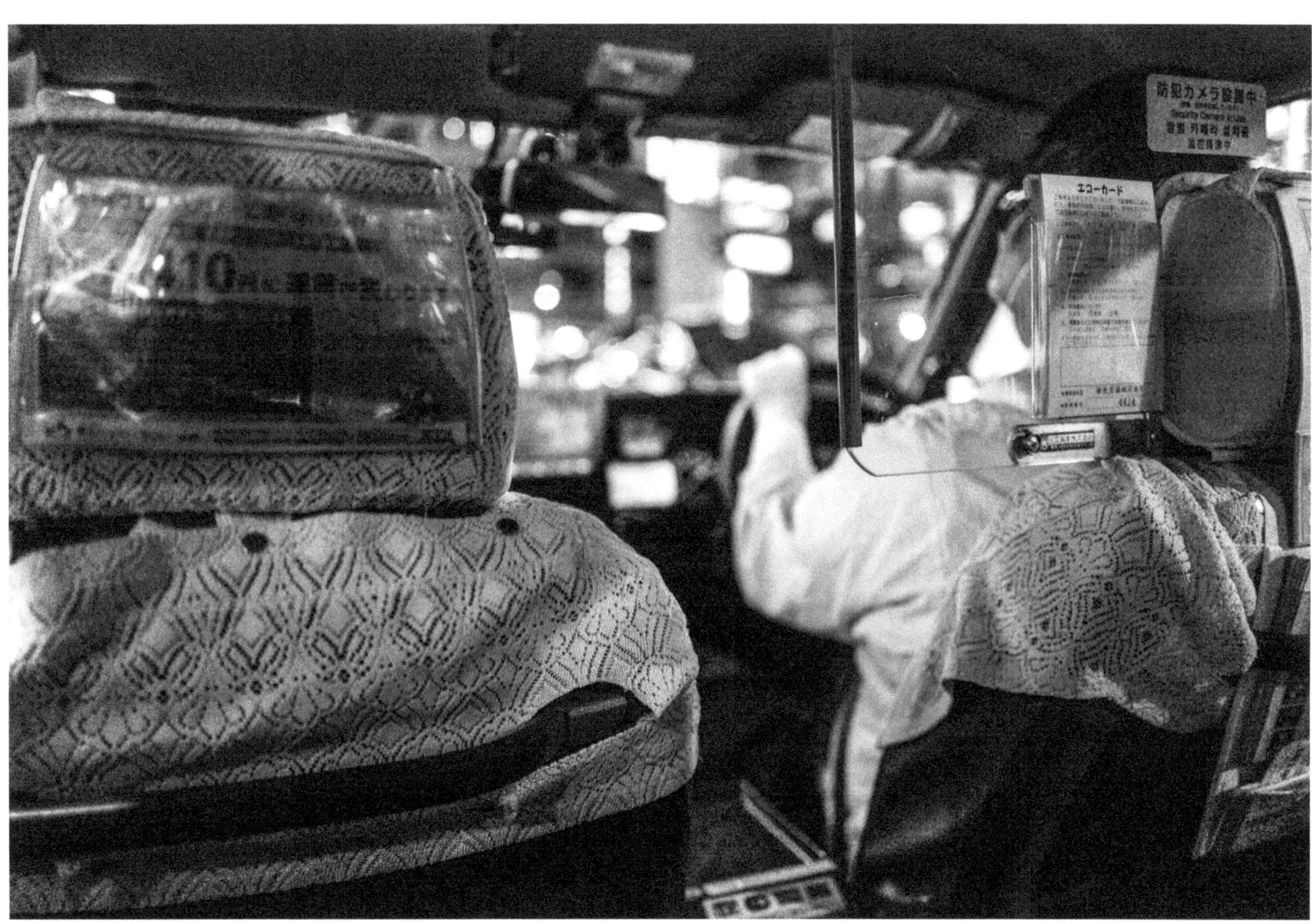
防犯カメラ設置中
Security Camera in Use
エコーカード

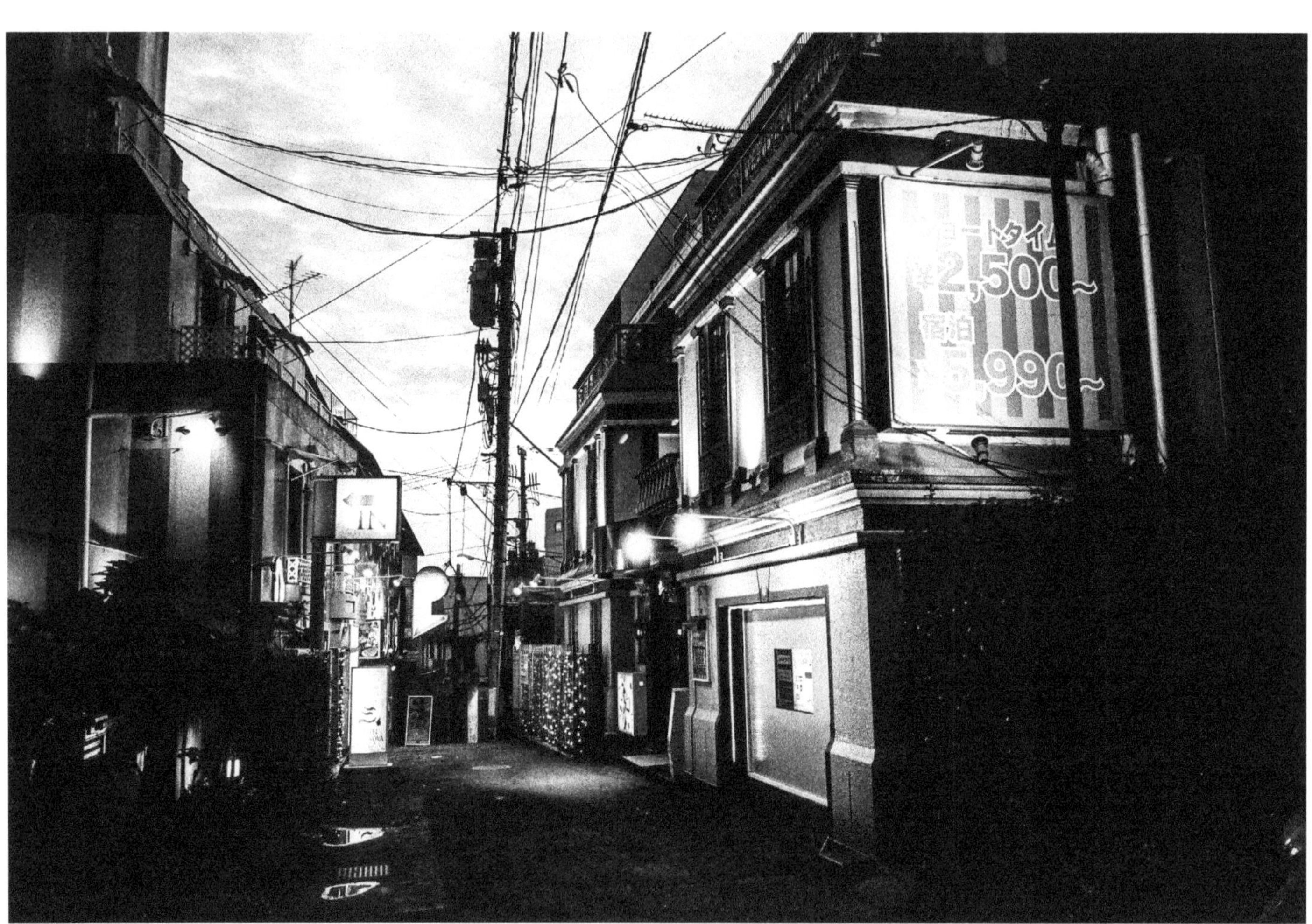
ートタイ
¥2,500~
宿泊
990~

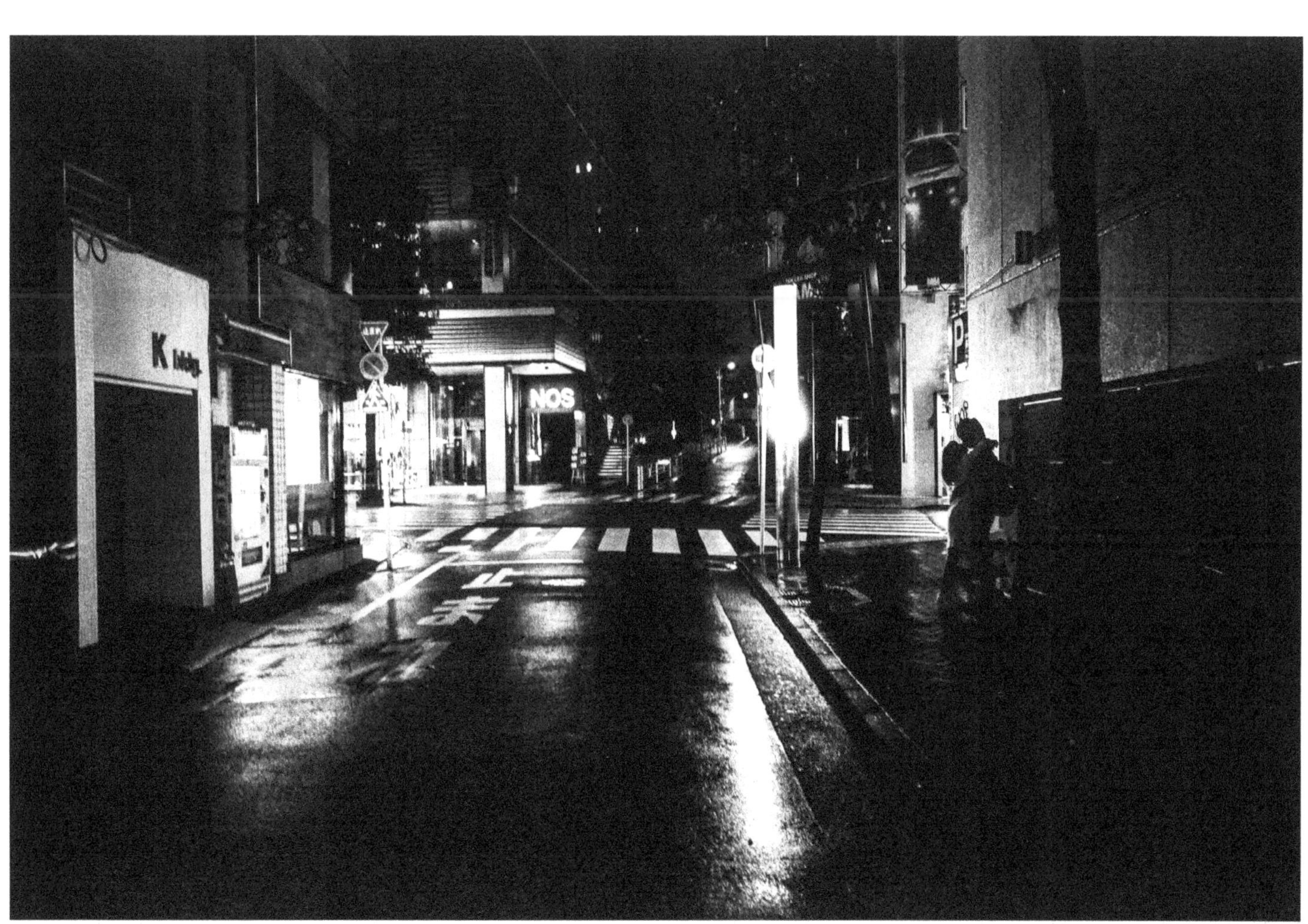
NOS

Tokyo is a great place to be left the fuck alone. My first trip to Japan, more than a decade ago, was an escape. I wanted, no… needed a change of scenery and for people to stop asking if I was OK. Unable to communicate with anyone, I spent my days walking aimlessly, headphones drowning out the city and reimagining my own soundtrack for it. I fell in love with it, with the idea of it. Physically close, emotionally distant. My quintessential romance – the object of my pining completely indifferent, while I'm left chasing something I can never touch. It was perfect.

Since then it's become a home and a sanctuary. A fortress of solitude filled with bodies. Like any other city with double digit millions of people you can find anything you want, you just have to look for it.

I look for the moments. Missed connections. Shadows of humanity. Proof of life. I don't always find it, but sometimes that works too.

It can sometimes take me weeks to finish a roll of film. I shoot it, throw it in a drawer, forget it. Eventually there are too many rolls in there so I gather them up and send them off to get developed. I don't remember which roll was shot when, or where. My archives are a disaster. I'm just as bad at downloading photos and do it a handful of times a year. I like the fresh eye and surprise I get when going through photos I forgot I'd taken.

Technical details: I shoot lots of Fuji Neopan, Some Kodak T-Max & TriX. 400, 1600 & 3200. Everything gets pushed. Over the last 10 years I've shot various film Leica Ms - 2, 6, 7, digital M Monochrom and Q. Mostly through 50mm Summilux & 28mm Elmarit. Lots recently with my Minolta CLE. I think it's the best M-mount film body you can get. I've started stockpiling them, If you have one you should give it to me. There may be a Rolliflex 3.5 appearance in here too.

Thanks to Tara for the endless support and encouragement, to Morgen for all the help and to coffee for obvious reasons.

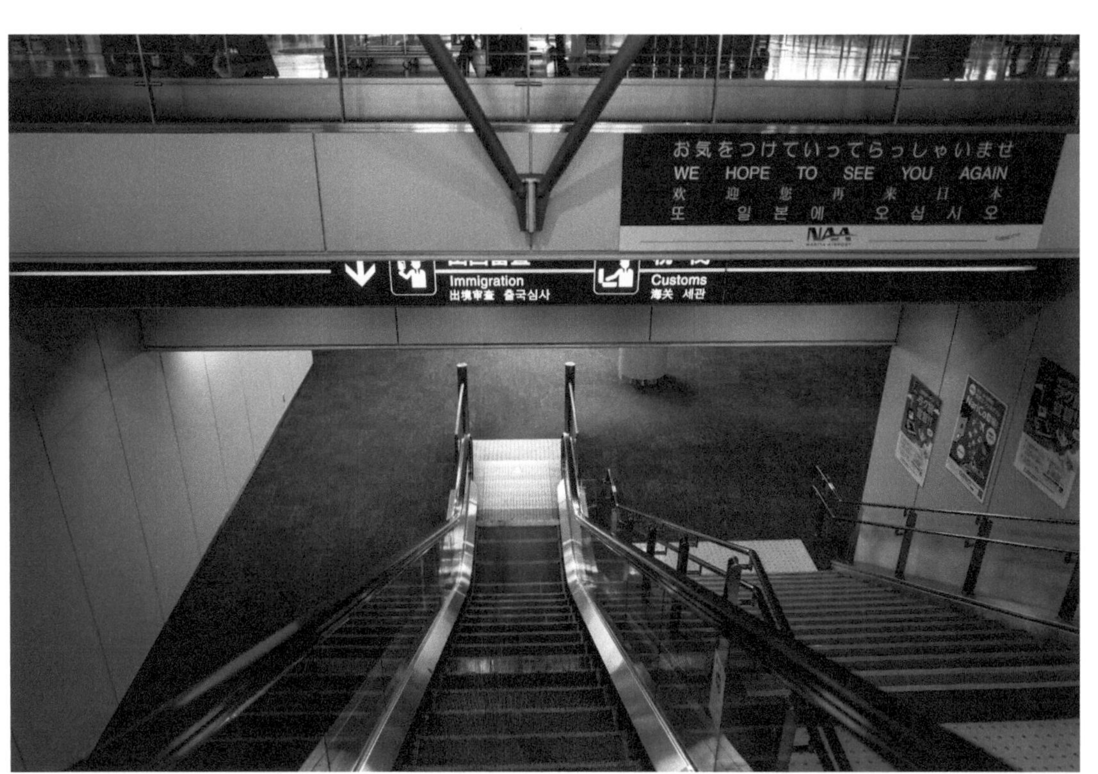
お気をつけていってらっしゃいませ
WE HOPE TO SEE YOU AGAIN
欢 迎 您 再 来 日 本
또 일본에 오십시오
NAA
Immigration
出境审査 출국심사
Customs
海关 세관

www.ingramcontent.com/pod-product-compliance
Lightning Source LLC
LaVergne TN
LVHW070149110826
845147LV00002B/357

* 9 7 8 0 9 8 9 8 1 4 4 3 0 *